anxious
for
nothing

YOUNG READERS EDITION

anxious *for* nothing

YOUNG READERS EDITION

Living Above Anxiety and Loneliness

BY MAX LUCADO

WITH ANDREA LUCADO

COVER BY OLGA BAUMERT
GRAPHICS BY MATTHEW WILSON

An Imprint of Thomas Nelson

Library of Congress Cataloging-in-Publication Data

Names: Lucado, Max, author. | Lucado, Andrea, author.
Title: Anxious for nothing: living above anxiety and loneliness / by Max Lucado with Andrea Lucado.
Description: Young readers edition. | Nashville, Tennessee, USA: Thomas Nelson, 2021. | Includes bibliographical references. | Audience: Ages 8–12 | Summary: "In this young readers adaptation of Anxious for Nothing, Max Lucado uses honest stories, relatable Bible study, and practical helps to encourage tweens to receive God's peace as they let go of anxiety, depression, and loneliness"—Provided by publisher.
Identifiers: LCCN 2021005710 (print) | LCCN 2021005711 (ebook) | ISBN 9781400229543 (paperback) | ISBN 9781400229550 (ebook)
Subjects: LCSH: Anxiety—Religious aspects—Christianity—Juvenile literature. | Worry—Religious aspects—Christianity—Juvenile literature. | Peace of mind—Religious aspects—Christianity—Juvenile literature.
Classification: LCC BV4908.5 .L793 2021 (print) | LCC BV4908.5 (ebook) | DDC 248.8/6—dc23
LC record available at https://lccn.loc.gov/2021005710
LC ebook record available at https://lccn.loc.gov/2021005711

Written by Andrea Lucado
Cover illustration by Olga Baumert
Interior graphics by Matthew Wilson

Printed in the United States of America

21 22 23 24 25 LSCC 6 5 4 3 2 1

Mfr: LSCC / Crawfordsville, IN / June 2021 / PO #12040402

Denalyn and I gladly dedicate this volume
to Rebecca Taylor—a portrait of courage
and joy in the midst of adversity.

Contents

Contents

SECTION 4: THINK ABOUT GOOD THINGS 115

Way to go! The fact that you have opened this book says a lot about you. I am so very proud of you for wanting an answer to this question: *How do I deal with worry?* Many people never seek that answer. They assume that anxiety comes with life. To a degree, they are correct. Anxiety comes with life. But anxiety shouldn't take over your life.

Good for you for working to get a hold on this problem before it gets a hold on you. I pray that God will use this book to equip you with tools for battling the enemy of worry.

Worry is when we let tomorrow's problems ruin today. There is nothing wrong with being prepared for tomorrow. Nor is it wrong to have a healthy concern for tomorrow. But worrying goes beyond preparation and healthy concern. Worry attempts to solve tomorrow's problems today. This is what led Jesus to say: "Don't worry about tomorrow, because tomorrow will have its own worries. Each day has enough trouble of its own" (Matthew 6:34).

Did you know the New Testament of the Bible was originally written in Greek? The Greek word for *worry* used in the Scriptures is a wonderful compound of two words that mean "divide" and "the mind." To worry, then, is to divide the mind. Anxiety splits our energy between today's plans and tomorrow's problems. Part of our mind is on the "now"; the rest is on the "not yet." The result is half-minded living.

How can a person deal with anxiety? You might try what a guy did in a story I heard. He worried so much that he decided to hire someone to do his worrying for him. He found a man who agreed to be his hired worrier for a salary of $200,000 per year. After he accepted the job, the first question the hired worrier asked his boss was "Where are you going to get $200,000 per year?" The other man responded, "That's your worry."

Sadly, worrying is one job you can't hire someone else to do for you. But worrying is a habit you can overcome.

With God as your helper, you will do just that. Again, I am so very proud of you! By discovering God's tools for dealing with anxiety, you will increase the odds of a happy and joy-filled life. May God open your mind and heart as you open His Word to receive His truth.

CHAPTER ONE

The Cloud of Anxiety

Have you ever felt worried about something big in your life? Have you ever felt worried about something small? Or have you ever felt worried for no reason at all—like the feeling you get when you know a thunderstorm is coming? You're afraid something bad is going to happen even though it hasn't happened yet. Maybe you get an upset feeling in your stomach. Or maybe it's a thought you can't stop thinking about.

When you feel worried like this, you are feeling *anxiety*.

When you feel anxious, you may not sleep well. Or maybe you don't laugh as much or enjoy being outside like you used to.

Anxiety brings a cloud over our heads, making life feel a little darker and a little scarier. Anxiety can also cause us to ask a lot of questions that start with these two words: *what if.*

What if I don't make any friends at school this year?

What if my teacher is rude?

What if my parents don't stop fighting?

What if I don't get to have a birthday party this year?

What if my phone gets taken away?

What if I don't make the team?

What kinds of "what if" questions do you ask? We all ask these kinds of questions. We all feel anxiety from time to time. Some of us feel it every day.

Anxiety Versus Fear

Anxiety is similar to fear, but these two feelings are quite different.

You feel fear when you know your body is in danger or someone else is in danger. Fear tells you, "Get out!" If you were walking outside and saw a rattlesnake on the ground, you would probably start walking (or running) away from the snake, right? That's because fear would tell you that you are in danger and need to get to a safe place. In this way, fear can be healthy. It protects you from bad things.

Fear tells you, "Get out!" Anxiety makes you ask, *What if?*

Anxiety causes you to ask, *What if?* That question can make you imagine all kinds of things you are afraid of that aren't really there. Fear tells you to run when you see a rattlesnake. Anxiety tells you to always feel afraid when you're outside because *what if* there's a snake?

See the difference?

Fear protects us from real dangers. Anxiety makes us think there's danger when there really isn't.

Where Is All This Anxiety Coming From?

The Bible says, "Worry is a heavy load" (Proverbs 12:25). Carrying worries through the day can feel like hauling a giant backpack up a mountain. Anxiety is such a heavy burden that it can harm our bodies as well as our minds. It can cause us to lie awake at night. It can cause our bodies to hurt or our stomachs to ache. It can make us feel sad and lonely.

Anxiety isn't fun.

Chances are that you or someone you know seriously struggles with anxiety. Doctors have found that one-third of teens ages thirteen to eighteen have an anxiety disorder. An anxiety disorder is when you feel a lot of anxiety a lot of the time. An anxiety disorder can make doing everyday things like going to school or a friend's birthday party feel hard or scary. Doctors also found that a lot of these teens started feeling anxiety at a younger age, usually around eleven years old and some as young as seven years old.

iGen: The Generation Growing Up Online

don't remember a time before smartphones existed

the generation born between 1995 and 2012

LOL

www.

spend 6-9 hours online per day

Like!

are experts at technology and social media

2004 | 2006 | 2008 | 2010

Loneliness in iGen

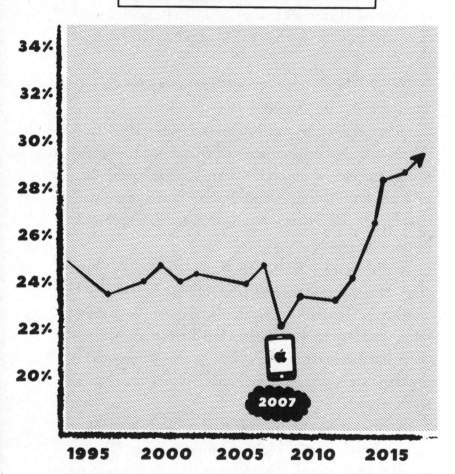

Some more bad news: the United States seems to be more anxious than other countries. We spend more money on medicine that treats anxiety, and we've reported more sicknesses caused by anxiety than other countries in the world.

Why? Why are we so anxious? There are a few reasons. One big source is technology.

Smartphones, the Internet, social media—all of these can make us feel extra anxious. In fact, at the time social media became popular, kids started going to the doctor more for problems related to anxiety and depression. (Depression is a constant feeling of sadness, which often happens because of anxiety.)

There are other reasons we might be anxious. Today, everything moves at the speed of a turbojet. Our ancestors didn't have the technology to build planes or fast cars, so they didn't travel much. Now we can drive to a new city or fly to a new country in hours. Things can change quickly when you are always on the go. That fast pace causes stress and anxiety.

Another reason we are so anxious has to do with information, how we get it, and how often we get it. Do your parents watch the news on TV or listen to it on a podcast or on the radio in the car? In our world today, we know what's going on everywhere all the time. We know about a war in the Middle East, a fire in California, a tornado in Alabama. Knowing about all of these things can cause us to worry.

Emma just got her first smartphone for her birth-day. This morning, Emma's parents told her she was allowed to download one social media app. She created a handle for herself, @BballEmma11, and started following four of her friends. When she got in the car to go to school, Emma checked her phone. Three of her friends had followed her back! But one hadn't. Emma began to wonder why this friend wasn't following her yet.

How would you feel if you followed a friend on social media but your friend didn't follow you back? Why might Emma's friend not have followed her back right away?

God's Promise

Sometimes as Christians, we can feel guilty for worrying. We know we are supposed to trust God, but we still feel anxious. Then, we feel guilty for feeling anxious. And that can make us more anxious! Are you feeling dizzy yet?

The Bible actually says a lot about anxiety and worry that can help us. Maybe you've heard of a guy named Paul in the Bible. A long time ago, right after the time Jesus lived, Paul wrote a lot of letters to churches to help them and encourage them as new Christians. These letters have been collected and are now in the New Testament of the Bible. One of these letters is called Philippians. Paul wrote it to a church in a city called Philippi.

In this letter, Paul wanted his friends to know they didn't have to worry about their lives because God was taking care of them. He wrote to them, "Be anxious for nothing" (Philippians 4:6 NKJV).

Do you think that's possible? To not feel anxious about *anything*?

Paul knew what it was like to feel anxiety. He had a pretty crazy life trying to share Jesus with the people around him and in other countries. Paul wasn't saying we should never feel anxious again. What he was saying is that we shouldn't feel anxious *all* the time. Because when we're anxious all the time, that feeling can take over our lives. And when that happens, it's hard to feel joy.

Anxiety is not a sin. It's an emotion.

We can't help feeling anxious sometimes. And let's be clear on this: anxiety is not a sin. It's an emotion. And our emotions aren't wrong. We often can't control how we feel, but we can control how we respond to our feelings. So anxiety is nothing to feel guilty about. Paul was simply telling Christians, "Don't let anxiety take over your lives."

Let's read more of what Paul wrote in Philippians 4:4–9:

Be full of joy in the Lord always. I will say again, be full of joy.

Let everyone see that you are gentle and kind. The Lord is coming soon. Do not worry about anything, but pray and ask God for everything you need, always giving thanks. And God's peace, which is so great we cannot understand it, will keep your hearts and minds in Christ Jesus.

Brothers and sisters, think about the things that are good and worthy of praise. Think about the things that are true and honorable and right and pure and beautiful and respected. Do what you learned and received from me, what I told you, and what you saw me do. And the God who gives peace will be with you.

You might have noticed that Paul gave us four instructions in this passage and one wonderful promise. That promise says, "God's peace, which is so great we cannot understand it, will keep your hearts and minds in Christ Jesus" (verse 7).

Let's look at the four instructions surrounding this promise:

1. Celebrate God. "Be full of joy in the Lord always" (verse 4).

Have you ever felt full of joy? What did your joy make you do? Maybe your favorite song came on, and you got up and danced. Or maybe you and your friend scored tickets to see your favorite band, and

C.A.L.M.

 1. **Celebrate God.**

2. **Ask God for help.**

3. **Look on the bright side.**

 4. **Meditate on good things.**

you were so excited you high-fived each other. When we are full of joy, we celebrate.

It's the same with God. When we remember who He is and what He has done, we can feel full of joy in a way that makes us want to celebrate Him through worship.

2. **Ask God for help.** "Pray and ask God for everything you need" (verse 6).

When we pray and ask God for help, we let Him take our worries from us. We don't have to carry them ourselves.

3. **Look on the bright side.** "Always giving thanks" (verse 6).

Remembering to thank God for the good things in our lives helps us see our situations with more positivity.

4. **Meditate on good things.** "Think about the things that are good and worthy of praise. Think about the things that are true and honorable and right and pure and beautiful and respected" (verse 8).

Meditate means to think about something with your full attention. When we meditate on good things, our brains and hearts feel more peaceful.

Calm.

Calm is what we need when we are anxious, right? God can give us calm.

God can give us calm.

God does not want you to feel anxious all the time. He made you for more than that. He wants you to live a life full of joy, and He is able to give that life to you. This doesn't mean you won't feel anxious, sad, or upset sometimes. But it does mean that, with God's help, you don't have to let those feelings rule your life.

Guarding the Door

When I was young, I remember my father loved to eat corn bread with buttermilk. (That might sound weird, but it was a West Texas specialty.) At about ten o'clock every night, he would walk into our kitchen and crumble a piece of corn bread into a glass of buttermilk.

Then he made the rounds to the front and back doors, making sure they were locked. Once everything was secure, he would step into the bedroom I shared with my older brother and say, "Everything is secure, boys. You can go to sleep now."

Now, I know God probably doesn't love buttermilk and corn bread like my dad did. But I know God loves His children. He looks out for you. He doesn't need to check if the doors are locked because He is guarding the door. He protects you from worry and fear.

Listen carefully. Hear Him say, "Everything is secure.

You can rest now." With God's help, you can be anxious for nothing. And you can have "God's peace, which is so great we cannot understand it."

Brain & Heart Check

At the end of each chapter in this book, there are activities and questions to help you check in with your thoughts (your brain) and your emotions (your heart). By completing these activities, you'll understand what anxiety is, how it affects you, and how you can work through it with God's help. Grab a journal or notebook, and start working on your worry!

We all feel anxiety in different ways. Underline or highlight all the statements that describe how you have felt in the last week.

My stomach hurt before I took a test or before another big event.
I had trouble sleeping because I couldn't stop thinking about a fear or problem.

My grades have dropped, and I have felt
distracted in class.
I felt angry at my parents or my siblings, and
I didn't know why.
I felt worried about things I didn't used to
worry about.
I got out of breath even though I wasn't
exercising.

If you marked any of these statements, you might have anxiety. Maybe you're only feeling a little bit of anxiety today. Maybe you've felt a lot of anxiety for several days in a row. Don't worry. Anxiety is completely normal.

There are two things you can do about your anxiety right now:

Share your anxiety with an adult you
trust. This could be a parent, teacher,
counselor, pastor, or another adult you
have a good relationship with. Let him
or her know how you're feeling.
Ask God for help. If you're not sure what to
say to God, use this prayer.

Dear Lord,
I know You are able to calm my heart and my

mind when I feel anxious. I feel anxious today, and I'm not sure what to do. Take my worries and my fears so I don't have to hold them anymore. In the Bible, You are called the Prince of Peace. Please bring me peace.

As I turn the pages in this book, teach me what I need to know about anxiety and Your strength and power. Help me with my anxiety. Give me courage. Help me have less fear and more faith.

In Jesus' name I pray, amen.

SECTION 1

Celebrate God's Goodness

Be full of joy in the Lord always.

—Philippians 4:4

CHAPTER TWO

Tent of Faith

I grew up in a family that loved to camp. My dad's idea of a great vacation was mountains, creeks, tents, and sleeping bags. Let others tour the big cities or go to theme parks. The Lucado family passed on Disney World and headed for the Rocky Mountains in Colorado.

My dad loved camping gear as much as he loved camping trips. One day when I was about nine years old, he returned from a trip to an outdoor store with a tent that became legendary in our family.

The tent was huge. It could hold a dozen people. We could raise the tent around a picnic table and still have room for our sleeping bags.

A big tent, of course, needs big tent poles to hold it up. This one came with two. But don't think these tent poles were the skinny ones that come with most tents.

These poles were made of cast iron and were as thick as a grown man's arm. Our tent wasn't fancy. We didn't have zippered doors or mosquito netting or a cool camouflage design. But it was a very sturdy tent. No wind, rain, or hail could get inside.

I remember going camping with my dad's family one summer in Estes Park, Colorado. My dad had eight brothers and sisters. It was a big group. One day the sky suddenly turned dark and stormy. Rain began pounding on us outside. The wind was so strong that the large pine trees bent under it. Everyone ran to their tents, but after a few minutes my aunts and uncles and cousins began piling into our tent because it was the biggest and the strongest. And with those big tent poles, they knew our tent wasn't going anywhere. We were safe, warm, and dry in there.

When we go through storms, we need a safe place to run to.

We go through storms in our lives all the time. But in these "storms," there is no rain or wind. These storms are emotional. They are the hard times in our lives when we get in fights with friends and family, when we don't make the soccer team, when our parents tell us we're moving to another city—again. These storms make us feel anxious. We need a safe place to run to, like my family's sturdy tent.

Joy No Matter What

Paul experienced a lot of storms in his life. His worst storm was probably while he was in prison in the ancient city of Rome. He was arrested for preaching about the power of Jesus. Paul's message that Jesus was both God and King threatened the government in charge during his day: the Roman Empire.

When Paul was in prison, he was about sixty years old. He had lived a hard life, traveling and telling people about Jesus. He often got in trouble for this. Members of the Roman army beat him. Some of his friends left him, no longer wanting to do the hard work of sharing the Good News of Jesus.

Even though Paul was in prison, he kept working for God. In jail he wrote the letter to the Philippians. Can you imagine writing "Be full of joy in the Lord always" when you are chained up and don't know if you'll ever be free? As he wrote, Paul knew that he could die in prison or be killed by the Romans.

But still, Paul wrote, "Be full of joy in the Lord always. I will say again, be full of joy" (Philippians 4:4). This is Paul's first instruction that will help with our anxieties: be full of joy in the Lord. And Paul didn't want us to rejoice in the Lord only one time or sometimes. What did he say? "Be full of joy in the Lord *always*" (emphasis added). And then, as if we didn't hear him the first time, he wrote, "I will say again, be full of joy."

Remember that when we are full of joy in the Lord, we can't help but celebrate Him. But how is it possible to celebrate God *all the time*? Sometimes we're sad and don't feel like celebrating. Sometimes we're anxious and don't feel joyful.

Let's talk about what it really means to celebrate God. It doesn't mean we get up and dance every time we think about Him. (But you can definitely do that if you feel like it!) It means we remember how good God is no matter what is going on in our lives.

In the Storm

There's a story in the Bible that can help us understand how to celebrate God in our storms. It's about a time when Jesus' disciples were out on a boat on a sea called Galilee. While they were on their boat, a crazy storm hit them.

Let's read the beginning of the story in John 6:16–18:

> That evening Jesus' followers went down to Lake Galilee. It was dark now, and Jesus had not yet come to them. The followers got into a boat and started across the lake to Capernaum. By now a strong wind was blowing, and the waves on the lake were getting bigger.

The hearts of these disciples began to sink like their boat was going to do if this storm didn't stop. They were soaked. Their voices were hoarse from yelling at each other over the sound of the storm. Their eyes looked afraid. They searched the sky, hoping to see a break in the clouds—a sign that the storm would end soon. They gripped the side of the boat every time a big wave hit. They screamed for help and prayed. But nothing happened.

If only Jesus were with them, they must have thought. But He wasn't. Jesus had told them to cross the sea and said He would catch up with them later. According to Mark 6:48, where this story is also told in the Bible, the disciples had probably been rowing from sunset until three in the morning by this point. This was not a fun trip on a lazy river at a water park.

What do you think the disciples were saying to each other during this storm?

"I'm not going to last much longer!"

"We're not going to survive this!"

Have you ever felt this way, like life was just too hard or scary or confusing?

Maybe it's been a tough few weeks at school, and it's not getting any easier. Maybe you didn't make the team. Then you didn't get a part in the school play. It just feels like nothing is going your way. Or maybe you're being bullied on social media, and you don't know what to do. You've tried to be kind, but it doesn't seem to be changing the bully's mind.

The disciples definitely knew how it felt to be in a tough spot. But let's read the rest of the story because it actually has a happy ending!

John 6:19 says, "They saw Jesus walking on the water, coming toward the boat. The followers were afraid."

You might have been frightened too if you were one of the disciples. Where did Jesus come from? How exactly was He walking on water? Were His feet hovering right above it? Was He riding the waves? Did the water split and create a path for Him? Was He walking on air? The Bible doesn't say, but you can use your imagination. And you can imagine this looked pretty amazing to the disciples.

Here's an interesting part of the story: Jesus came to the disciples *while* the storm was still happening. Jesus doesn't wait until the hard time is over to be with us. He is with you right now, in the middle of the disaster.

When Jesus saw that the disciples were afraid of Him, He yelled: "It is I. Do not be afraid" (John 6:20). Jesus assured the disciples, they didn't need to be afraid because He was with them.

After the disciples heard Jesus say, "It is I. Do not be afraid," Scripture says, "They gladly took him aboard, and at once the boat reached the shore they were making for" (John 6:21 PHILLIPS). Right when Jesus showed up, the disciples were safely on the other side of the sea!

That's how powerful it is to have Jesus in the storm with us. His presence can quiet and calm. So even if our storm keeps going, we can feel peace when we remember Jesus is with us.

What are you afraid of right now that Jesus could help you with? You can trust Him to take care of it. Just as He told the waves to quiet and the wind to stop tossing the boat, He will bring peace to your storm.

So no matter what is happening around you—a hurricane, an illness, or trouble with a friend—remember to celebrate that God is there with you. And He will help you get through it.

Tent Poles

Paul never stopped celebrating God. He remembered what God had done for him, even when he was in prison. His faith was like the sturdy tent my dad bought. The cast-iron poles of Paul's belief in God kept his soul stable. Friends could abandon him. Citizens could kick him out of town. Soldiers could knock on his door. But Paul's tent of faith would never collapse. He had stabilized it with a sturdy belief system. Is your faith strong like that?

What you believe about God can tell you how strong and sturdy your faith is. Your belief system answers the basic questions about life: Is anyone in control of the universe? Does life have a purpose? Do I matter? What happens after death?

Your belief system has nothing to do with your skin color, appearance, talents, or age. Your belief system is

> **What you believe about God can tell you how strong and sturdy your faith is.**

not made of the outward things people can see but of the inner things in your heart. It's these things, these poles of belief, that your faith depends on. If your poles are strong, you will stand. If they are weak, the storm will knock you down.

Take a close look at the poles in Paul's tent of faith. One belief that comes up a lot in Paul's writing is this: God is sovereign. *Sovereignty* describes God's perfect control and management of the universe. He is in charge, and He is involved in all of His creation. He directs the world toward fulfilling His great purpose.

When it comes to anxiety, understanding God's sovereignty is huge. We often get anxious when we feel like we don't have control over our situations. It's like you are in the ocean but don't know how to swim. The waves are tossing you around.

We tend to worry about things we can't control. You can somewhat control your grades by how hard you work. But even then, you might have a hard time with a certain subject. Or maybe you try to control your body with how much you eat or exercise. But everyone's body is unique, so you'll never be able to look exactly like that social media influencer or that actor. (And that's okay!) Things like politics, the environment, and racial justice are big and important, but we don't have much power over them. When we wish we had control of something in our lives but don't, we start to feel anxious.

What Kids Worry About

world problems

friends

appearance

making mistakes in front of peers

the environment

popularity

grades

health of loved ones

the future

being laughed at

His Steady Hand

So what do we do? Should we try to control everything in our lives? Maybe you've tried that before. How did it work out? When we try to control everything we're anxious about, it can make us even more anxious!

For example, if you're afraid of planes, you might try to control that anxiety by never getting on a plane. Or if you're afraid of getting in a car accident, you could try to control that anxiety by never getting into a car. Or maybe you're afraid you won't be able to make friends at school, so you never go to school. Trying to control anxiety and what you're anxious about can make life sad and no fun.

The Bible tells us what we can do with the things we can't control. Instead of trying to control them, we should let them go. Remember Paul's promise? "God's peace, which is so great we cannot understand it, will keep your hearts and minds in Christ Jesus" (Philippians 4:7).

Peace doesn't come once you get control of everything in your life. (Because that will never happen!) Peace comes when you build your tent of faith with God's poles. Believe that God is sovereign. Trust Him with your worries and anxieties. You can feel peace even though you don't have control of everything—because God does have control. What a relief!

Paul trusted God's sovereignty. He wrote: "What has happened to me has helped to spread the Good News. All the palace guards and everyone else knows that I am in prison because I am a believer in Christ" (Philippians 1:12–13). Even from a jail cell, Paul could see that God had a purpose for his life.

Oliver likes to watch soccer highlights and videos about animals on YouTube. But yesterday, he watched a news video on the home page. The video showed a protest in a big city near where Oliver lives. The footage showed people yelling at one another, but Oliver wasn't sure why they were upset. When he went to bed that night, he kept thinking about the people in the video. It was hard for him to fall asleep.

Have you ever felt anxious about something you saw online that you didn't understand? If you were Oliver, what would you do to feel less anxious?

Paul's writing in the Bible shows that he was convinced of the steady hand of a good God. He was protected by God's strength. He was cared for by God's love. He lived beneath the shadow of God's wings.

Do you?

The next time you fear the future, remind yourself to be full of joy in God's sovereignty. Remember what He

As your belief in God gets bigger, your anxiety will get smaller.

has already done for you. Celebrate that He is able to do what you cannot do. Fill your mind with thoughts of God like these from Scripture:

"[He is] the Creator, who is blessed forever" (Romans 1:25 NKJV).

"[He] is the same yesterday, today, and forever" (Hebrews 13:8).

"[His] life will never end" (Psalm 102:27).

God is your creator. He does not change. He stays the same. And He will always be in control. These beliefs are the strongest tent poles you can find. And as your belief in God gets bigger, your anxiety will get smaller.

Brain & Heart Check

1. What "storm" or hard time are you going through right now? Or what storm have you been through in the past?
2. How did this storm make you feel?
3. This image is your tent of faith. The tent poles are your beliefs. Write on the poles what you

believe about God. Color the tent with your favorite colors, and draw a design on it. What does your tent of faith look like?

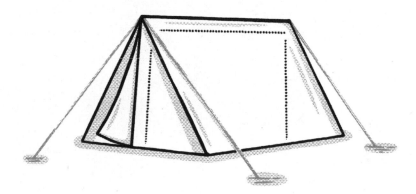

CHAPTER THREE

Celebrate God's Mercy

Have you ever felt guilty about something you did? Maybe you hit your younger sibling, or you lied to your parents, or you watched something on TV you weren't supposed to watch. We all mess up sometimes, and when we do, we often feel guilty.

Guilt is the feeling inside you that says, "I did something bad." It feels bad, but guilt can be a good thing. It keeps us from hurting ourselves and others.

Yet there is a feeling darker and deeper than guilt that says, "I *am* bad." This feeling is called shame, and shame isn't healthy. Guilt is a feeling that goes away once we confess the bad thing we did or once we feel forgiven for it. Shame is a feeling that sticks with us for a long time.

Shame makes us feel bad about ourselves. It makes us think we don't deserve good things. And it can make us feel like we're not enough—not cool enough, not smart enough, not pretty enough, not athletic enough.

A lot of the girls Emma follows on social media wear makeup and pretty clothes. They take selfies that make them look like movie stars. Emma has never cared about girly stuff before. She likes to wear comfortable clothes she can play basketball in. And she's not allowed to wear makeup yet. But when Emma looks at the photos in her feed, she feels like maybe she isn't pretty enough or girly enough. She's started to think about buying nicer clothes and wearing makeup in her selfies.

What should Emma do to help her feel good about her looks?

That feeling of not being enough can make us feel anxious. We start to worry about how we *can* be enough. Should we work harder? Should we wear different clothes? Should we stay at basketball practice longer?

These are anxious questions that come from shame.

Have you ever felt shame? What made you feel that

way? Was it something you did? Or was it something someone else said to you? Did feeling shame also make you feel
anxious?

You aren't alone in feeling shame. We've all felt it.

The Beginning of Shame

People have experienced shame from the very beginning.
Adam and Eve were the first people God created. Adam
and Eve lived in a garden called Eden. This garden had
everything Adam and Eve needed: food, animals, and
beautiful flowers and plants.

God told Adam and Eve that they could eat the
fruit from any tree in the garden except one: the Tree of
Knowledge of Good and Evil. Adam and Eve did as God
told them. They didn't eat from that tree until . . . Eve
met a snake in the garden. The snake told Eve she should
try the fruit from that tree. The snake said it would give
her knowledge of things only God knew. Eve believed the
snake and ate the fruit. Then Eve gave some of the fruit
to Adam.

But as soon as they ate the fruit, something inside them
changed. They felt shame for the first time. When they
heard God's footsteps in the garden, they tried to hide.

Shame makes us want to hide like Adam and Eve did.
It's such a bad feeling, we just want it to go away. So we try
to hide from it. Maybe when you feel shame, you want to

hide under your bed, or in a closet, or behind a tree in the backyard.

We do other things to get away from our shame. We try to distract ourselves by playing lots of video games or looking at social media for a long time. Or we try to pretend we aren't feeling shame, so we push the feeling deep down and hope we won't feel it anymore.

Or we might punish ourselves for feeling shame. We can do this by telling ourselves mean things in our heads like, *I'm dumb. I'm ugly. I'm not smart. I'm not funny.* Sometimes shame can even make us want to hurt ourselves physically. Maybe you or someone you know has cut his or her own skin. This is called self-harm. There are a lot of reasons people might self-harm, but shame is one of them.

When Faith Crumbles

Shame is a powerful emotion. If we're not careful, it can take over our lives. But God doesn't want us to feel shame. One story in the Bible shows particularly well how God wants to free us from shame.

Peter was one of Jesus' disciples. Peter and Jesus were close. They lived together, traveled together, prayed together, and ate together for three years.

But Peter wasn't perfect. Far from it.

Before Jesus died, He knew the cross was coming. He also knew that many of His disciples would run away when the horrible event occurred. Jesus told the disciples that they would all stumble in their faith. But Peter didn't believe Him:

> Peter said, "Everyone else may stumble in their faith, but I will not."
>
> Jesus answered, "I tell you the truth, tonight before the rooster crows twice you will say three times you don't know me."
>
> But Peter insisted, "I will never say that I don't know you! I will even die with you!" And all the other followers said the same thing.
>
> —Mark 14:29–31

But Jesus was right. Peter's faith crumbled the night before Jesus died. When soldiers came to arrest Jesus, the other disciples ran. Peter followed behind in the shadows. He wanted to know what would happen to Jesus, but he made sure not to be seen by the soldiers. The soldiers took Jesus to a trial. Peter stayed outside in the courtyard and sat around a fire with some other people.

> While Peter was in the courtyard, a servant girl of the high priest came there. She saw Peter warming himself at the fire and looked closely at him.
>
> Then she said, "You also were with Jesus, that man from Nazareth."
>
> But Peter said that he was never with Jesus. He said, "I don't know or understand what you are talking about."

Then Peter left and went toward the entrance of the courtyard. And the rooster crowed.

The servant girl saw Peter there, and again she said to the people who were standing nearby, "This man is one of those who followed Jesus." Again Peter said that it was not true.

A short time later, some people were standing near Peter saying, "Surely you are one of those who followed Jesus, because you are from Galilee, too."

Then Peter began to place a curse on himself and swear, "I don't know this man you're talking about!"

At once, the rooster crowed the second time.

—Mark 14:66–72

It all happened like Jesus said it would.

When Peter realized what he had done, he "lost control of himself and began to cry" (verse 72).

What do you think Peter was feeling in this moment? Have you ever been caught gossiping about a friend or saying something mean about someone you love? How did it make you feel when you were caught? You probably felt shame like Peter felt when the rooster crowed.

But that wasn't the end of Peter's story.

Second Chances

Three days later, Jesus rose from the dead. He found His disciples on a boat, fishing on the Sea of Galilee. The disciples saw someone standing on the shore, but they didn't recognize Him at first.

Then Peter realized it was Jesus: "The follower whom Jesus loved said to Peter, 'It is the Lord!' When Peter heard him say this, he wrapped his coat around himself. . . . Then he jumped into the water" (John 21:7).

Peter dove into the sea, swam to shore, and climbed up on the beach. Just a few days earlier, Peter had pretended he didn't know Jesus. Now, he was so excited to see Jesus, he couldn't wait for his boat to get to land!

We might expect Jesus to let loose on Peter. It wouldn't surprise us if Jesus reminded Peter of the betrayal and the broken promise. Jesus could have called down every "I told you so" from heaven. Peter certainly deserved it.

But no. Jesus simply said this: "Come and eat" (John 20:12).

Who would have imagined this invitation? Just days earlier, Jesus had died to pay for the sins of all humans. He knocked out the Devil and treated the grave like a hotel. Holding confetti and lining up for a pearly gate victory parade, heaven's angels were ready to celebrate. But the party would have to wait.

Jesus wanted to eat breakfast with His friends. He saw the layers of shame on Peter's heart. And as if with a cotton swab of grace, He began to wipe the shame away.

After breakfast, Jesus asked Peter, "Do you love me more than these?" (verse 15).

In my imagination, Jesus waved toward the other disciples as He asked the question. Peter had announced his devotion before: "Everyone else may stumble in their faith, but I will not," he had boasted in Mark 14:29. But Peter did stumble. He denied the Lord three times on the night that Jesus was arrested. Three days later, the Lord responded with three questions:

"Do you love me more than these?" (John 21:15).
"Do you love me?" (verse 16).
"Do you love me?" (verse 17).

Peter took the opportunity to repent of each denial with a confession.

"I love you" (verse 15).
"I love you" (verse 16).
"I love you" (verse 17).

Each time, Jesus gave Peter a direction:

"Feed my lambs" (verse 15).
"Take care of my sheep" (verse 16).
"Feed my sheep" (verse 17).

Jesus had work for Peter to do, people for Peter to pastor. The apostle was discouraged, but he was not disqualified from doing God's work.

Jesus gave Peter a second chance, and He will give you a second chance. No matter how much shame or guilt you feel, go to Jesus. He will give you another chance.

Get Unstuck

God gives us second chances because He loves to show His children mercy. *Mercy* is another word for forgiveness or compassion. God's forgiveness is a gift for us. He forgave all of us when He sent His Son Jesus to die on the cross, and He forgives each of us every day for little and big mistakes we make. So when you feel anxious because of your shame, celebrate God's mercy!

God's mercy is big and deep and wide. And God's mercy is for everyone—not just good and perfect people. (Hint: Perfect people don't exist!) He shows mercy to anyone who asks Him for it.

So don't get stuck in shame and the anxiety that grows around it. When we trust God's mercy to forgive us, our anxiety goes away. We can feel joy again. We feel free. And we are ready for a second chance. When we don't trust God's mercy, we can get even more stuck in our shame and anxiety.

God's Mercy Is Bigger

God's mercy changed my life. In high school and in college, I made a lot of bad choices. I hung out with the wrong crowd. I did things just because everyone else was doing them. Even though I was a Christian, I still did things I regretted.

For years, I lived with guilt over the things I did. The shame weighed me down. I felt bad about who I was and the choices I was making. But then I went to church one day and heard a preacher tell me what I've been telling you: God's mercy is bigger than our sins.

God's mercy is bigger than our sins.

At the end of his sermon, the preacher asked if anyone would like to come forward to receive God's mercy. I ran to the front in the same way Peter swam to Jesus. I was so tired of the shame that I didn't care what anyone else who saw me thought. I wanted the forgiveness this preacher was talking about.

That was forty years ago! (Yes, I'm old.) Since then, I have certainly felt anxious at times, but you know what? I don't feel anxious because of my shame anymore. I am a sinner, but I have received mercy.

Even though I've sinned and made mistakes since that day at church, I know God doesn't love me any less. He's not giving me any less mercy or forgiveness. These gifts are still mine to keep.

A Very Sticky Mess

When I was young, my older brother and I were playing tag in the grocery store while my mom shopped. Even though she had told us to behave, we didn't listen. We were running around the store and not being careful. I remember running around a corner so fast that when I came up to a big table of honey, I couldn't slow down. I slid right into the display, and glass jars of honey shattered all over the floor. It was a very sticky mess.

The store manager came around the corner to see what all the noise was about. When he saw me, he asked, "Whose boy are you?"

I froze right there on the floor. I looked at the honey all around me. I looked at the angry store manager. I was sure I would be sent to prison or something really bad for what I had done. But just then, I heard a voice behind me. It was my mom.

FIGHT SHAME WITH GOD'S TRUTH

When you feel . . .	Remember God says . . .
I'm not good enough. ⟹	He will help me (Isaiah 41:10).
There's something wrong with me. ⟹	He created me just right (Psalm 139:13–14).
I don't belong. ⟹	I am His child (1 John 3:1).
I'm a bad person. ⟹	He will forgive me (1 John 1:9).

"He belongs to me," she said. "We'll clean up this mess."

My mom took responsibility for me and my mess. Jesus does that too. He took responsibility for all of our messes when He died for our sins on the cross. Because He gave His life, we are forgiven. No matter how much of a mess we get ourselves into, He will always claim us as His own and forgive us. With Him on our side, we are safe.

And we don't have to do anything to earn this mercy from God. Remember, mercy is a gift, and gifts are free!

This reminds me of a family of trapeze artists known as the Flying Rodleighs. When an interviewer asked one of the flyers the secret of trapeze artists, the acrobat said:

> The secret is that the flyer does nothing and the catcher does everything. . . . When I fly to Joe [my catcher], I have simply to stretch out my arms and hands and wait for him to catch me and pull me safely over the [swing]. . . .
>
> The worst thing the flyer can do is to try to catch the catcher. I am not supposed to catch Joe. It's Joe's task to catch me. If I grabbed Joe's wrists, I might break them, or he might break mine, and that would be the end for both of us. A flyer must fly, and a catcher must catch, and the flyer must trust, with outstretched arms, that his catcher will be there for him.

In the great trapeze act of salvation, God is the catcher, and we are the flyers. We trust. Period. We trust God to catch us. As we do, a wonderful thing happens: we fly.

Brain & Heart Check

1. Do you worry about being good enough? Ask an adult to help you find a Bible verse that tells what God says about you. Memorize the verse and recite it to yourself the next time you feel like you're not good enough.
2. Write five things you like about yourself. And remember, God made you just the way He wanted you!
3. Is there anything you need forgiveness for? Don't let shame grow. Say you're sorry to the person you hurt and ask God to forgive you.

Be Full of Joy *Always*

I want you to do something kind of strange. Place your fingers on each side of your forehead and say this prayer: "Thank You, Lord, for my amygdalae. Thank You, Lord, for this part of my brain. I wouldn't be alive without it."

Amygda . . . what?

Your amygdalae (pronounced uh-mig-duh-lee) are two small, almond-shaped parts of your brain located behind your forehead. They are your body's alarm system. In a house, an alarm system sounds when an intruder is near. The alarm is there to tell you, "Get out! Get to a safe place! A bad guy is near!"

The amygdalae sound an alarm whenever you are in danger. If you are crossing the street and a car honks its horn, your amygdalae tell you: "Step back on the sidewalk!

Get out of the way!" If you're hiking in the woods and see a bear, your amygdalae will tell you: "Run!" If you're at a baseball game, and a foul ball is coming at your head, your amygdalae will tell you, "Duck!"

We are able to react quickly when faced with danger because of the warning system of our amygdalae.

When our amygdalae are on high alert, they tell our bodies to get ready to protect ourselves. We breathe faster to get more oxygen. Our pupils dilate to make our vision better. Our pulses race to pump more blood in our veins. We become faster and stronger, ready to escape danger. Pretty cool, huh?

Our amygdalae sound an alarm anytime our bodies are in danger.

But our amygdalae can be *too* sensitive. When they are, they can cause us to overreact and become anxious when there isn't any real danger. For example, let's say you fall off your bike and scrape your knee. It's not a bad injury, but your overactive amygdalae might say, "Bikes are dangerous! Never ride one again!" Or let's say you get a bad grade on a test. It's just one test, and you can always do better next time. But your overactive amygdalae say, "You failed! Drop out of school!"

Constant anxiety happens when your brain's alarm system never quite turns off. Some anxiety is helpful. We need to be alerted to danger. But we don't need to live in a state of high alert.

Are You Anxious?

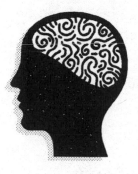

You feel **worried** often, and you're not sure why.

You look for **danger**.

You imagine worst-case scenarios.

You feel **tense** or jumpy.

You're irritable.

You have trouble **focusing**.

Your mind goes blank.

Your heart beats fast.

You **sweat**.

You have an upset stomach.

You feel **dizzy**.

You have to go to the bathroom a lot.

You have a hard time breathing.

You get **headaches**.

You can't sleep at night.

Shutting Off the Alarm

Do you have overactive amygdalae? If you feel jumpy, worried, or irritated a lot, you might need to retrain your brain to be calm except when there's real danger. Sound like a big job? Don't worry. God will help you, and His Word gives you just the right place to start!

Remember that in Philippians 4:4 Paul wrote: "Be full of joy in the Lord always." *Always*. Not just on Fridays or your birthday. But be full of joy *always*.

When the World Turns Gray

Joseph understood how hard it was to feel joy when life was difficult. Joseph's story is in the book of Genesis. He lived about twenty centuries before Paul did, but they both knew the challenge of being in prison.

Joseph had dreams that showed what was going to happen in the future. He was also good at interpreting what dreams meant. One night he had a dream that his brothers were bowing down to him as if he were a king and his brothers were his servants. When he told his brothers about the dream, it made them angry. They wanted to get rid of him, so they sold him as a slave.

Joseph ended up in Egypt as a slave to a rich man named Potiphar. But Potiphar's wife didn't like Joseph. She accused him of a crime he didn't commit. That's how he ended up in prison. Joseph's jail was dank and dark, a dungeon of windowless rooms. He dined on only stale food and bitter water. He had no way out.

And he had no friend to help him. Although at first, he thought he did. In jail, Joseph met a man who had been a butler in Pharaoh's palace. He interpreted a dream for the butler, telling him he would soon be serving Pharaoh again. Joseph asked the butler to put in a good word for him. The butler agreed. Joseph's heart raced; his hopes soared. He kept an eye on the jail door, expecting to be released any minute.

"But the officer who served wine did not remember Joseph. He forgot all about him" (Genesis 40:23). So had everyone else, it seemed. Joseph was completely abandoned.

Joseph ended up being in prison for two years! Two years for a crime he didn't commit. That's plenty of time for the world to turn gray. Plenty of time for him to wonder, *Where is God? Is this how He treats His children? Is this His reward for good behavior?*

We don't know if Joseph asked such questions. But he might have. I would have.

Have you ever asked questions like that? Have you ever gone through a time so hard it left you wondering if God cared or even knew what was happening to you?

A lot of people think God doesn't care. Or they don't believe there is a God because they reason that if there was one, life wouldn't be so hard. But Christians believe that God is real and that He cares what happens to us. Hebrews

1:3 says, "The Son reflects the glory of God and shows exactly what God is like. He holds everything together with his powerful word."

This verse means that Jesus is holding the world and directing it in a certain way. He isn't making things up as He goes along. He has a plan. But if God has a plan, why do bad things happen to us? Why have bad things happened to people we love? Why are some days really hard? Let's talk about the rest of Joseph's story to find out.

"But God"

Remember the palace butler Joseph met in prison? Well, he eventually remembered Joseph when Pharaoh had some scary dreams. The butler remembered that Joseph was good at knowing what dreams meant. Pharaoh called Joseph to the palace. Joseph told Pharaoh the dreams were a warning. A drought was coming to Egypt, and the nation would run out of food. Pharaoh was so impressed that he pulled Joseph out of prison and hired him. Joseph became Pharaoh's right-hand man and helped the people store up enough food so they could survive the drought.

Years later during the drought, Joseph's brothers came to Egypt to buy food. When the brothers discovered Joseph, they expected him to be angry and arrest them. But Joseph said, "You meant to hurt me, but God turned your evil into good to save the lives of many people, which is being done.

So don't be afraid. I will take care of you and your children" (Genesis 50:20–21).

There are two very important words in these verses: *but God*.

Joseph said, "You meant to hurt me, *but God*..." Joseph had a good perspective on his life. He knew he had suffered a lot. But he also knew God had been with him in the middle of that suffering, working on a plan for good—actually, a plan to save thousands of people from starvation!

Life is hard, but God is good and He cares.

If we forget that God is with us working toward good things during our hard times, we can grow anxious. Knowing God is in control and cares about our lives brings us peace. Life is hard, *but God* is good and He cares.

Saying "but God" can help you with the things you're worried about. Look at these examples:

> My parents are getting a divorce, but God cares about me and is a good Father.
> My grandmother is sick, but God knows this and He loves my grandmother.
> I'm failing English class, but God is with me even when I fail.

This is how God can calm our amygdalae. When our amygdalae try to tell us to freak out or worry, we can say, "But God _____." Just fill in the blank for any situation.

One night before bed, Oliver was looking at his friends' pictures on social media. One friend posted a photo of her and another classmate in the library studying for a test. Oliver was in the same class as these friends, but he hadn't started studying for this test yet.

When he saw his friend's picture, he got worried. Should he have started studying sooner? Was he going to fail? The girls in the picture were some of the smartest girls in his class. He started to feel dumb for not studying sooner. He started to worry he would get a bad grade. Then he worried it was too late to catch up.

Have you ever felt anxious about a test or a project at school? What would you tell Oliver to help with his anxiety?

It Is Finished

Joseph's life is a good example of God using a bad situation for good. But Jesus' death and resurrection are the best examples.

No deed was more evil than Christ's crucifixion. No other day was so dark. But the crucifixion was the key event in God's plan ever since Adam and Eve sinned in the garden. As Peter told the Jews a few weeks after Jesus' death: "This man was handed over to you by God's deliberate plan and foreknowledge; and you, with the help of wicked men, put him to death by nailing him to the cross. But God raised him from the dead, freeing him from the agony of death, because it was impossible for death to keep its hold on him" (Acts 2:23–24 NIV).

Did you catch it?

But God had a plan.

The last thing Jesus said before He died was "It is finished" (John 19:30). Jesus had come to do a job: save us. Luke 19:10 says, "The Son of Man came to find lost people and save them."

When Christ died on the cross, He was the payment for our sins. The work of Christ on the cross means anyone who follows Jesus gets to be in heaven one day with God. Our sins will not keep us from getting there. Jesus took care of that. It is finished.

While Jesus' death was painful and sad for His friends to see, it was not pointless. God had a plan. It also wasn't the end of Jesus' story. He rose from the dead three days later! The religious leaders and Romans tried to hurt Jesus, *but God* had a plan.

Joseph's and Jesus' stories teach us that we have a choice about how we respond to the hard times in our lives. We can either let our amygdalae take over and soak us in anxiety, or we can say:

But God has a plan.
But God loves me.
But God is taking care of this.

When we focus on His plan, God gives us peace that calms our anxiety.

It Is Well

Some time ago I made a special visit to the American Colony Hotel in Jerusalem. I was in Israel with a long list of places to visit and sites to see. But at the top of the list was a visit to the lobby of this hotel. I didn't place it on my list just because I am an American. And I didn't want to go just because the food in the restaurant is tasty and the hotel is nice. I wanted to see the handwritten lyrics that hang on the wall, framed for all to see.

Horatio Spafford wrote these lyrics, never imagining they would become the words to one of the world's most famous hymns.

In 1871 Horatio and his wife, Anna, suffered tragic losses in the Chicago fire. In November 1873, Anna and their children set sail for Europe with a group of friends. Horatio stayed home to take care of some business. On

December 2, he received a telegram from his wife that said, "Saved alone. What shall I do?"

He soon learned that the ship had collided with a British vessel and had sunk. Their four daughters had drowned. Only Anna had survived. He left for England to bring Anna back home. As the ship crossed the ocean where his children had died, he wrote the lyrics to a song that proclaimed God's wisdom and care in the middle of suffering. It's called "It Is Well with My Soul." Maybe you've heard of it. May we trust in God so that we can also say, "It is well with my soul." Always.

Brain & Heart Check

1. Draw a cartoon strip of a time when your amygdalae protected you. What was the danger?
2. Draw a cartoon strip of a time when your amygdalae overreacted to something. What did your brain think was dangerous? Do you often feel anxious about that "threat"? Ask God for help with this fear.

3. Underline or highlight any of these things that you've experienced recently:

stomachache

difficulty breathing

heart racing

headache

sweating when still

difficulty falling asleep

trouble focusing

forgetting things

feeling tense or jumpy

imagining disasters

4. The next time you experience one of these things, come back to this section and complete these sentences.

I am _____.

I am worried about _____.

But God _____.

Ask God for Help

Pray and ask God for everything you need.

—Philippians 4:6

CHAPTER FIVE

Contagious Calm

In 1962, four Russian submarines sailed to the coast of Florida. The submarines had been on a long, rough journey, and the men inside were tired. They had hit a hurricane that caused them to ride fifty-foot waves. They sailed through warm ocean waters that caused the temperature in their submarines to rise to 120 degrees.

The Russian men were exhausted, anxious, and tired of being cooped up inside hot submarines. Then, they found out American ships were following them. The Russians thought they were under attack.

The captain of the submarine fleet lost his cool. He gathered his staff and pounded the table with his fists. "We're going to blast them now! We will die, but we will sink them all—we will not disgrace our Navy!"

During this time, Russia and the United States did not get along. An attack could have caused a third world war. But then an officer named Vasili Arkhipov asked for a moment with the captain. The two men stepped to the side. Vasili urged the captain to reconsider. He suggested they talk to the Americans before reacting. The captain listened. His anger cooled.

The Russian submarines eventually dove down deep underwater where the American ships couldn't see them. Then they sailed safely home to Russia.

That day, one calm man stopped a war from starting. His calm affected his captain, and countless lives were saved. One historian said, "The lesson from this [event] is that a guy named [Vasili] Arkhipov saved the world."

You might be wondering why I'm sharing this story with you. You're not in the navy. You've probably never been on a submarine. But you know what it's like to be stressed. You know what it's like to have a hard class or a coach who yells at you or a parent who is sick. You know what it's like to be under pressure like the Russians on that submarine.

When we're in situations like this, it's tempting to lose our temper and get angry. Or to make decisions too quickly like the Russian captain tried to do. It's tempting to lose our calm, lose control, and do something we regret. Have you ever done this? Maybe you were stressed about school and snapped at your younger sister when she asked you a question. Or maybe you said something mean to a friend or

A Calm Person...

Prays before acting.

Listens to others.

Treats others with **kindness**.

Considers the **facts** before reacting.

 Speaks gently.

Looks for the **solution** that is best for everyone.

Tries to see others' points of view.

Keeps their cool.

Assumes the **best** about people.

Trusts God to work out problems.

Be quick to listen, slow to speak and slow to become angry.
-James 1:19 *NIV*

yelled at your mom or were disrespectful to your dad. We all do things we regret when we're stressed and anxious. But we can learn to be calm like Vasili Arkhipov, even when life around us is not.

You Are Never Alone

This is the way of living that Paul called for in Philippians 4:5–6: "Let everyone see that you are gentle and kind. The Lord is coming soon. Do not worry about anything."

Do you know anyone who is gentle and kind? Someone who speaks softly, who says kind things to others, who doesn't get angry often? We are drawn to people like this. They help calm us down when we're stressed. We feel safe around them. Paul tells us we should all be gentle and kind so others will notice.

Vasili Arkhipov's gentleness calmed down the submarine captain. Calm is contagious. If you have a cold, you are contagious. You stay away from friends and family so they won't catch it. Calmness works in the same way, except it's a good thing to spread! When you are around a person who is calm, it makes you calmer. You catch their contagious calm.

A person who has contagious calm reminds others, "God is in control." It's the captain of the football team who says, "Don't worry. We're losing now, but we'll catch up." It's the teacher who reminds you, "The test will be difficult, but you are smart and prepared. You can handle it." It's the type of person who makes you feel calm in the face of something that usually makes you feel anxious.

How can you become one of these people? Just look at our verse again: "The Lord is coming soon. Do not worry about any-

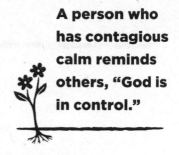

A person who has contagious calm reminds others, "God is in control."

thing." Another translation of this verse says, "The Lord is near. Do not be anxious about anything" (NIV).

The Lord is near! You are not alone. You may feel alone, but God is with you in every moment.

Just look at some of these verses from the Old Testament.

God told Isaac, "Don't be afraid, because I am with you" (Genesis 26:24).

He told Joshua, "Don't be afraid, because the LORD your God will be with you everywhere you go" (Joshua 1:9).

God even calls himself Immanuel, which means "God with us." And God became flesh and bone just like us when Jesus came and lived on the earth. God couldn't get any closer than that! And now we have the Holy Spirit, who is God's spirit. The Spirit comforts and guides us.

Bread and Fish

Because the Lord is near, we don't have to worry about anything. Even when we feel as if we are drowning under tasks, expectations, and just *life*, He is there. And He is able

One Saturday afternoon, Emma texted with a few friends. One of them shared a post from their school's social media account announcing basketball tryouts for next year. Emma really wanted to make the team. Playing basketball is one of her favorite things to do.

Her friends wanted to make the team too. One of them messaged: "I am sooooo nervous! I heard there's gonna be a new coach, and she's super intense."

Another friend chimed in: "Oh no! I should've practiced more over the summer. My piano lessons are taking up too much time. Maybe I should quit!"

Emma's friends kept talking about how nervous they were about tryouts. It made Emma's stomach hurt. She hadn't been that nervous before, but now she was getting more and more anxious about try- outs. And they were still several months away!

Have you ever been caught up in a conversation like this? Your friends start talking about some- thing, and before you know it, you feel nervous or anxious about something you weren't worried about before. What message could Emma send her friends that would be gentle and kind? How could she spread contagious calm?

to handle all of those things that make us feel overwhelmed.

You know the feeling. You know the fear that freezes your brain when the information is too much to learn. Or the change is

Because the Lord is near, we don't have to worry about anything.

too great to make. Or the options are too many to choose from. Or the sadness is too deep to see past. Or the mountain is too tall to climb. Or the crowd is too many to feed.

At least that is what the disciples told Jesus. Have you heard the story? Let's look at John 6:1–4:

> After this, Jesus went across Lake Galilee (or, Lake Tiberias). Many people followed him because they saw the miracles he did to heal the sick. Jesus went up on a hill and sat down there with his followers. It was almost the time for the Jewish Passover Feast.

At a certain point Jesus realized that the crowd had nothing to eat. They had no more food in their sacks, and they were out in the country. The gospel of Matthew, which also tells this story, says there were five thousand men in the crowd, plus women and children. There were probably more than fifteen thousand people there! And they were *all* hungry.

> When Jesus looked up and saw a large crowd coming toward him, he said to Philip, "Where can we buy

enough bread for all these people to eat?" (Jesus asked Philip this question to test him, because Jesus already knew what he planned to do.)

Philip answered, "Someone would have to work almost a year to buy enough bread for each person to have only a little piece."

Another one of his followers, Andrew, Simon Peter's brother, said, "Here is a boy with five loaves of barley bread and two little fish, but that is not enough for so many people."

—John 6:5–9

How did Philip and Andrew respond? Philip was negative, saying it would be impossible to get enough money to buy food for all the people. Andrew said the five loaves and fish the little boy had offered wasn't enough. And he wasn't wrong. What the boy had was definitely not enough, but the disciples were forgetting one thing. They were in the presence of Jesus. They had been following Him around for a while now. They had watched Him teach, do miracles, and be so incredible that fifteen thousand people had gathered to listen to Him that day.

Yet Philip, a practical guy, looked out over the sea of faces. He heard the murmurs and imagined the grumbling stomachs. And he replied with no hesitation: "We ain't got what it takes to face this challenge. Our wallet hasn't got the cash. There are too many mouths and not enough dollars."

Note that each person talked about the overwhelming number of people in need of food:

Jesus' question: "Where can we buy enough bread for all these people?" (verse 5).

Philip's response: "Someone would have to work almost a year to buy enough bread for each person to have only a little piece" (verse 7).

Andrew's idea was to start with the boy's meal. But then he said: "That is not enough for so many people" (verse 9).

Jesus acknowledged "all these people." Philip saw no help for the feast it would take to offer "each person" a bite. Andrew had an idea, but the suggestion wilted in the face (or faces) of "so many people."

Have you felt like that? Your big challenge might be "all this homework" or "all these fights" or "all these illnesses." Whatever it is, the need is far greater than the supply. You feel as hopeless as Philip and as small as Andrew.

We'd like to think that Jesus' followers would respond with more faith. Before this day, they had seen Him . . .

heal leprosy (Matthew 8:3),

calm a storm (Matthew 8:26),

heal a paralyzed man (Matthew 9:6–7),

heal a woman who had been sick for twelve years (Matthew 9:22),

and raise a girl from the dead (Matthew 9:25).

They counted the hungry people, the money in their bag, and the amount of bread and fish. They did not, however, count on Christ.

And He was standing right there! He could not have been nearer. They could see, hear, touch, maybe even smell Him. Yet the idea of asking for His help did not dawn on them.

Even so, Jesus went right to work.

Jesus said, "Tell the people to sit down." There was plenty of grass there, and about five thousand men sat down there. Then Jesus took the loaves of bread, thanked God for them, and gave them to the people who were sitting there. He did the same with the fish, giving as much as the people wanted.

When they had all had enough to eat, Jesus said to his followers, "Gather the leftover pieces of fish and bread so that nothing is wasted." So they gathered up the pieces and filled twelve baskets with the pieces left from the five barley loaves.

—John 6:10–13

I imagine the people sprawled out on the green grass, so full and satisfied that they needed a nap. Hungry bellies became happy bellies. There was so much food that there were twelve baskets of leftovers. The impossible challenge of feeding "all these people" became the unforgettable miracle of all these people fed.

This is what happens when we ask Jesus for what we need. Our problems are never too big for Him. He is never overwhelmed. What we cannot do, Christ does!

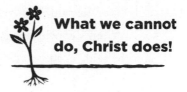

What we cannot do, Christ does!

Tree Stumps

In a book called *The Dance of Hope*, author William Frey shares a story from when he was eleven years old. William grew up in the country in Georgia. One of his chores was gathering firewood for the small wood stove in his family's house. He would search the woods for stumps of pine trees that had been cut down. Then he would chop the stumps into kindling for his family to burn.

> One day I found a large stump in an open field near the house and tried to unearth it. I literally pushed and pulled and crowbarred for hours, but the root system was so deep and large I simply couldn't pull it out of the ground. I was still struggling when my father came home from his office, spotted me working, and came over to watch.
>
> "I think I see your problem," he said.
>
> "What's that?" I asked.
>
> "You're not using all your strength," he replied.
>
> I exploded and told him how hard I had worked and for how long.

"No," he said, "you're not using all your strength."

When I cooled down I asked him what he meant, and he said, "You haven't asked me to help you yet."

Calming anxiety is a lot like pulling tree stumps out of the ground. Some of your worries are rooted deep down inside of you like the roots of a tree. Taking them out is hard, hard work. But you don't have to do it alone.

Tell God what your challenge is. Ask for help.

Will He solve your problem? Yes, He will.

Will He solve it immediately? Maybe. Or maybe He'll solve it later or in a way you didn't expect. Either way, He is with you right here, right now. And when you give Him your worries, He will give you contagious calm.

Brain & Heart Check

1. Think of someone you know who is gentle and kind. How does that person treat and speak to others? How could you be more gentle and kind like this person?

2. Sometimes we have worries that last a long time. These worries are like the roots of a

tree: they run deep down inside us. Write
your biggest worries into the tree roots in the
picture.

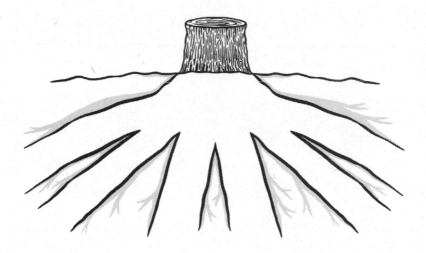

3. Now ask God to help you with all of these
   rooted worries. If you're not sure what to say,
   use this prayer:

Dear God,

*Sometimes my worries feel so big, and I feel
so small. These are things I've worried about for
a long time. I think about them all the time, and
I'm not sure what to do.*

*But I know You are able to perform miracles.
You can heal people. You can help with friend-
ships and relationships. I need Your help today,
God. I give all of these worries to you. Please take*

care of them. Calm my anxiety. Give me con-tagious calm so that I feel peaceful and bring calm to everyone around me. In Jesus' name, amen.

CHAPTER SIX

Prayer, Not Despair

What was the last thing you asked your parents for? When my daughters were young, they didn't say things like "Please be a good father to me today." They asked specific questions like "Can you pick me up from my friend's house after school?" Or "I left my lunch at home. Can you bring it to me?"

They asked for exactly what they needed. We can do this with God in prayer. We can give as many details as we want, about anything and everything. He listens to each word.

Paul said in Philippians 4:6, "Do not worry about anything, but pray and ask God for everything you need, always giving thanks." Until now, Paul has told us to take comfort in who God is. God is merciful. God is

Peace happens when people pray.

sovereign. God is near. Remembering these things about God brings us comfort when we feel anxious. Now in this verse, Paul has called us to act!

Prayer is where we get to work. It's a way for us to deal with our worries. It's choosing to take worries to God before anxiety can take over. Peace happens when people pray.

God wants us to pray about everything. As Paul said, "Do not worry about anything," but pray about "everything."

Everything? Does God really want us to pray about everything? Even a scraped knee or that argument we got into with a friend or that game we have coming up? Does God really care about all that stuff? Yes!

PRAYER TIPS

1. Pray everywhere.
2. Give God your worries for the day when you wake up.
3. Pray about everything, small and big.
4. Tell God exactly what you need.
5. Keep praying until God answers—no matter how long it takes.

No Request Is Too Small

God wants to hear about your tiniest wishes and smallest problems. Let's read what happened when someone asked Jesus for something pretty unimportant in John 2:1–5:

> Two days later there was a wedding in the town of Cana in Galilee. Jesus' mother was there, and Jesus and his followers were also invited to the wedding. When all the wine was gone, Jesus' mother said to him, "They have no more wine."
>
> Jesus answered, "Dear woman, why come to me? My time has not yet come."
>
> His mother said to the servants, "Do whatever he tells you to do."

Mary asked her son to deal with the problem: empty wine containers. Folks in first-century Israel, where Jesus lived, knew how to throw a party. A wedding and reception didn't last for just one day. Weddings lasted as long as seven days. Food and wine were expected to last just as long. So Mary was worried when she saw the party had run out of wine.

We don't know why they ran out of wine, but we know how they got more. Mary presented the problem to Jesus. Jesus wasn't sure He should help at first. But Mary had confidence He could solve the problem. So she told the servants to do whatever Jesus told them to do. Nearby there were six huge stone water jars that the Jews used in their washing ceremony. Jesus took action.

> Jesus said to the servants, "Fill the jars with water." So they filled the jars to the top.
>
> Then he said to them, "Now take some out and give it to the master of the feast."
>
> So they took the water to the master. When he tasted it, the water had become wine. He did not know where the wine came from, but the servants who had brought the water knew. The master of the wedding called the bridegroom and said to him, "People always serve the best wine first. Later, after the guests have been drinking awhile, they serve the cheaper wine. But you have saved the best wine till now."
>
> So in Cana of Galilee Jesus did his first miracle. There he showed his glory, and his followers believed in him.
>
> —John 2:7–11

Had I been at the wedding, I would have stopped Mary from asking Jesus to help. "He was not sent to the earth to handle such basic, day-to-day tasks," I would have told her. "He is saving His miraculous powers to raise people from the dead, cast out demons, and heal lepers. Not fill up empty wine bottles."

But I was not there that day, and it's a good thing. Because as it turns out, our requests can never be too small for God.

Do you ever want to pray about something but think God won't care? Remember this story. It was a small problem, but Jesus fixed it. And He didn't just fill up a couple of wine bottles. Scripture says there were six stone jars that held 20 or 30 gallons of water each. Jesus turned all of that water into wine. That's up to 180 gallons of wine!

Jesus cares about your small requests, and He can answer them in a big way.

Jesus cares about your small requests, and He can answer them in a big way.

A GU-ey Problem

I have a story that proves God cares about our prayer requests, no matter how small they are. Several years ago, I trained to run a half-IRONMAN triathlon. This is a serious race. First, you swim 1.2 miles, then you bike for 56 miles, then you run 13.1 miles.

Anyone who does this race knows they have to bring snacks with them. We're on the racecourse for six hours. We get hungry. One of the popular snacks is called GU. It fits in a little package and is made of a gooey substance that gives you lots of energy. I always bring plenty of GU in my pockets, but during this race I ran out. I still had a long way to go, and I knew I needed more GU if I was going to finish.

Oliver has started to wonder if he's spending too much time online. He feels anxious whenever he's been on his phone late at night. Then he checks his feed more and more throughout the day. And it bothers him when he can't check. During class and family dinners, he worries he's going to miss something important or that someone will leave a mean comment. He wants to use the Internet and social media in a good way, but he isn't sure how.

In Sunday school this week, his teacher talked about prayer. His teacher said they could pray for anything and God would listen. Oliver wonders if he should ask God about how much time he should spend on his phone and on the Internet each day. But Oliver feels silly asking God for something like that. Usually when he prays, he prays for his grandma who is sick. He knows God cares about his grandma and her health. But he isn't sure God cares about social media.

Do you think Oliver should pray about this situation? If you do, what could Oliver say to God?

So you know what I did? I prayed for GU. That might sound strange. I've prayed some serious prayers in my life. I've prayed for people who were sick and people who were dying. I've prayed for babies right after they were born. I've prayed for broken hearts. But I had never prayed for GU. What was I to do? I needed the GU!

So I prayed while I ran. I said, "Lord, this might be the only time You've heard this prayer request, but here is my situation. I ran out of GU, and I need more to get me through this race."

Did the GU fall from heaven? Well, kind of. I only knew three other people who were in this race. Three out of thousands. One was a friend from Indiana. And guess who ran up beside me just as I was praying for GU? Yep, that friend from Indiana.

"Hey, Max, how's it going?" he asked me.

"Well, I have a problem," I told him.

When he heard I needed GU, he reached into his pocket and pulled out three packets.

"Here," he said. "I've got plenty!"

You might be thinking this is a weird story. You have real problems, bigger than running out of GU. But that's my point!

Why did Jesus agree to Mary's request for more wine? No one was dying. It wasn't an emergency. He did it because Mary cared about it. He cares about your problems too—no matter how small—because you care about them. If He can take care of my GU, imagine what He can do for you.

Why Do People Pray?

People pray for different reasons.

 **64%**
to communicate with God

 **57%**
to worship God

 55%
to ask for help in hard times

 47%
to help anxiety

People pray for different things.

 **75%**
for the people in their lives

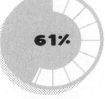 **61%**
for their country

 **33%**
for people they don't agree with

Everything You Need

Paul told us to pray for everything we need. When we do this, three things happen.

1. We show God that we are serious about our prayers.

   If you tell a friend, "Hey, can I come to your house sometime?" that friend might not think you're serious about coming over. But if you ask your friend, "Can I come over on Friday afternoon?" then your friend will know you really want to come over.

   It's the same when we pray. When we tell God exactly what we need, He knows we mean it.

2. We are able to see how God works.

   This is kind of like my GU story. I knew God had answered my prayer because I prayed for GU and I got it. When you pray for something specific, it's easy to see how God answers your prayer.

3. We don't carry around as much worry.

   Sometimes we feel anxious, but we don't stop to identify what we're anxious about. We're just keeping the feeling inside. This can make it hard to know exactly what is making us feel worried.

   Maybe you feel worried every time your dad comes home from work. You're not sure why; you just do. If you sat with God and really talked to Him about that worry, you might realize your dad comes home from work stressed about the meetings he had all day. His stress makes you feel stressed. When you realize this, you can pray to God, "Help my dad not feel so stressed, and help me understand that when he is stressed, it's not my fault."

I try to pray every morning before work so I don't carry around too much worry. I get really detailed in my prayers, saying things like, "God, I have a meeting at 10:00 a.m. that I'm worried about. Will You help me know what to say and how to respond to others?" Then if I worry about that meeting when I get to work, I remember that I already gave this worry to God. He's got it, and I don't have to worry about it anymore.

Give All Your Worries to Him

In 1 Peter 5:7, the Bible says, "Give all your worries to him, because he cares about you." This is what I try to do in the mornings before work. You can do it too. Before school or before a game or before anything you're worried about, give your worries to God in prayer. And tell Him *exactly* what you need.

I did this with my algebra teacher when I was in school. I was not good at math, and math class always made me feel worried. But my algebra teacher told us at the beginning of the year, "If you cannot solve a problem, come to me, and I will help you."

I did exactly what he said. Every time I couldn't figure something out, I walked straight to my teacher's desk, and he helped me. I did this probably a hundred times throughout the school year. Each time my teacher helped, and we solved the problem together.

You can do this with God. Anytime you have a problem, take it to Him. He will help you solve it.

Brain & Heart Check

1. Paul tells us to ask God for everything we need. What do you need today? Make a list of everything you can think of.
2. Now, pray about the things on your list. Tell God every detail.

For later:

3. Did God answer any of your prayers? If He did, how?

Look on the Bright Side

Always giving thanks.

—Philippians 4:6

CHAPTER SEVEN

Say "Thank You"

The widest river in the world is not the Mississippi, the Amazon, or the Nile. The widest river in the world is a river called If Only.

Crowds of people stand by this river all the time. They look at it and wish they could get to the other side. There, they believe, all their wishes will be granted. If Only isn't a real river, of course. But in the same way rivers separate us from one side of a piece of land, our wishes separate the life we have from the life we want.

How would you fill in this blank? If only ____.

I were more popular.

I were the team captain.

I were prettier.

I were smarter.

There is nothing wrong with hoping for things to get better. But sometimes our wishes make us worry. We think that if we could just have a fairy godmother come grant all our wishes, *then* we would be happy.

But happiness doesn't work this way. The more wishes we have, the less happy we are. And the more worried we become.

Our friend Paul told us that the "good life" doesn't begin when our lives change. It begins when our attitude toward our lives changes. He said, "Do not worry about anything, but pray and ask God for everything you need, always giving thanks" (Philippians 4:6).

The "good life" begins when your attitude changes.

Let's look at those last three words: *always giving thanks*. Whenever we pray the words *help me*, *forgive me*, or *show me*, we should also be praying these two words: *thank You*.

An Attitude of Gratitude

When we say "thank You" to God, we express our gratitude to Him for the blessings in our lives. *Gratitude* is an *attitude* of thankfulness. This attitude of gratitude helps us be C.A.L.M. by looking on the bright side.

Looking on the bright side doesn't mean pretending

the bad things in our lives don't exist. It just means that we change where our minds spend the most time. We focus on the good rather than the bad. We focus on what we're grateful for instead of what we wish for.

Doctors and researchers have found that gratitude can improve our lives in many ways. Grateful people are kinder to others and more forgiving. People who keep a gratitude journal, where they 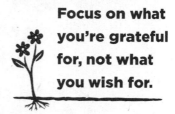 **Focus on what you're grateful for, not what you wish for.** write down what they're thankful for, have a more positive outlook on life. Grateful people are less jealous, they care less about material things, and they are less focused on themselves. Gratitude helps people feel better about themselves. It helps people sleep better, and it improves their relationships.

Gratitude is like medicine for the soul. It makes everyone feel better!

One reason has to do with the If Only river. When we are grateful for what we have, we stop saying "If only ____." Instead we feel at peace with our lives—even if everything isn't going our way. When we're at peace with ourselves and our lives, we feel less anxious. We stop feeling like we need to change ourselves or that the people around us need to change or that our lives need to change. When we practice gratitude, we feel peace and joy no matter what's happening around us.

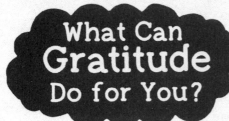

What Can Gratitude Do for You?

gratitude *(grat·i·tude)* **noun.**
A positive feeling toward good things and people in your life.

Gratitude improves...

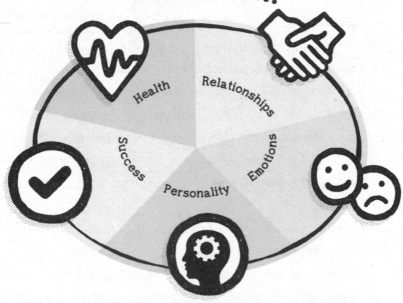

Health

Relationships

Success

Emotions

Personality

Keeping a daily gratitude journal changes how we feel.

10%

happiness

15%

optimism

15%

satisfaction with life

17%

hope

13%

negative emotions

15%

depressed feelings

Count Your Blessings

My friend Jerry is a great example of someone who is content because he is grateful. His wife, Ginger, has an illness called Parkinson's disease. Parkinson's disease makes it hard for Ginger to move around. Jerry has spent a lot of time in the hospital with her.

Jerry could feel sad or angry, but he doesn't. You know why? Every morning he and his wife sing a hymn together. Jerry always asks Ginger which one she wants to sing, and she always wants to sing an old hymn called "Count Your Blessings." When they are done singing, they do what the hymn says and remember all the good things in their lives.

When we focus on our blessings, no matter how hard life is, our attitude toward life gets brighter.

Take a second to count your blessings right now. Think about what you are thankful for. Your family? Friends? A good breakfast? Your blessings can be big or small. All of it counts as gratitude.

The Secret to Contentment

Paul figured out how to be content with his life, even when things weren't going his way. And that was a lot of the time.

He wrote in Philippians 4:11–13: "I have learned to be satisfied with the things I have and with everything that

GRATITUDE JOURNAL TIPS

Are you ready to feel happier, more peaceful, and less worried? Start a gratitude journal. You can write in a blank notebook, type on your computer or phone, or even make a video journal. However you choose to journal, follow these tips to get the most out of an attitude of gratitude.

1. Be specific as you record your blessings.
2. Journal about only a few things at a time, and think deeply about those things. Why are you thankful for these gifts? How do they make you feel? How do they make your life better?
3. Include people in your journal. Studies have found that being grateful for people has a larger effect on our overall happiness than being grateful for things.
4. Record events that surprised you.
5. Use categories as prompts. For example, one day write about relationships you are thankful for. Another day, write about the simple things in your life, such as the sun's glow, clean clothes, or spaghetti. Write about an opportunity, a kindness, or a skill. On the first page of your journal, make a list of categories you can refer back to.

happens. I know how to live when I am poor, and I know how to live when I have plenty. I have learned the secret of being happy at any time in everything that happens, when I have enough to eat and when I go hungry, when I have more than I need and when I do not have enough. I can do all things through Christ, because he gives me strength."

Remember, Paul wrote this while he was in prison. A guard was constantly watching him. He wasn't going to be set free anytime soon. He had every reason to complain, but instead he said, "I have learned the secret of being happy at any time in everything that happens" (verse 12).

What was his secret? Read that last sentence again: "I can do all things through Christ, because he gives me strength." The secret to contentment is leaning on Jesus and what He's done for you!

If your happiness depends on how many social media followers you have, home runs you make, or As you receive in class, your happiness will go up and down all the time. You'll be happy when you get new followers and sad when you lose them. You'll be happy when you get a good hit and sad when you don't. You'll be happy with an A and disappointed with a B or C.

But when your happiness depends on Jesus, you can be happy all the time. Because you have Jesus all the time.

Paul didn't focus on what he didn't have while he was in jail: friends, good food, play time, freedom. Instead, he focused on what he did have: Jesus. And in Jesus he had an entire list of amazing things: salvation, forgiveness, grace, love. What he had in Christ was far greater than what he didn't have in life.

Raised from the Dead

Like Paul, you can count on Jesus for forgiveness, grace, love, and salvation because of Jesus' resurrection. The resurrection is the foundation of the Christian faith.

After Jesus died, two of His followers, Joseph of Arimathea and Nicodemus, got Jesus' body from the Romans (John 19:40–41).

> These two men took Jesus' body and wrapped it with the spices in pieces of linen cloth, which is how they bury the dead. In the place where Jesus was crucified, there was a garden. In the garden was a new tomb that had never been used before.

Joseph and Nicodemus prepared Jesus' body for burial. They knew He was dead. He didn't have a pulse. They closed the tomb behind them. They said their goodbyes.

But the next morning, something happened: "Early on Sunday morning, while it was still dark, Mary Magdalene came to the tomb and found that the stone had been rolled away from the entrance" (John 20:1 NLT).

Jesus was crucified on a Friday. He lay in the tomb all day Saturday. On Sunday, He was gone. What had happened? Did someone take His body? Mary Magdalene, one of Jesus' followers, thought so. She ran to Jesus' disciples Peter and John and said, "They have taken the Lord out of the tomb, and we don't know where they have put him" (John 20:2).

John and Peter raced to the cemetery. John was faster, but Peter was bolder. He entered the tomb first and came out bewildered. Then John entered the tomb and came out believing. "Then the other follower, who had reached the tomb first, also went in. He saw and believed" (verse 8). Jesus had told His disciples that He would rise from the dead on the third day (Mark 8:31, 9:31, and 10:34). Friday, the day He died, was day one. Saturday was day two. Now it was Sunday—day three.

John remembered and believed. No one had stolen Jesus' body. He had risen from the dead.

Paul said, "If Christ has not been raised, your faith is worthless and powerless" (1 Corinthians 15:17 AMP). Since He has been raised, we can continue the thought: our faith is true, precious, and powerful. We can count on the blessings of being His followers: His forgiveness and a home in heaven. We can count on His presence in our lives and His death-destroying power in the middle of our hardest moments.

When this is your good news, what could bring you down?

Emma has a pretty good life. Her parents are kind, and they love her. Emma shares a room with her sister, but she has her own bed. They have a TV in the living room and a laptop to share. Some of her friends from school live in her neighborhood, so she can play with them whenever she wants. Life is pretty good for Emma.

But when she's on social media, Emma sometimes wishes for more. One of her friends went on a beach vacation over the summer. Emma's never been to the beach. Another friend posted about going shopping with her mom for new school clothes. Emma's mom doesn't take her shopping often, especially if her clothes still fit. One of Emma's friends posted about getting her ears pierced. Emma isn't allowed to get her ears pierced yet.

These posts make Emma want more clothes, cooler vacations, and pierced ears. They make her life seem plain and unexciting.

What can Emma do to feel better?

Living Is Christ

To Paul, what he had in Christ was all that mattered. Within the 104 verses of Philippians, Paul mentioned Jesus forty times. That's every two and a half verses. As he said, "To me the only important thing about living is Christ, and dying would be profit for me" (Philippians 1:21).

Paul's only goal was to know Jesus. He didn't care about being rich. He didn't care about being famous. All he wanted was more of Christ. And Christ was with him at all times, so Paul was content.

Brain & Heart Check

1. What are you worried about today? List anything you can think of.
2. What are you thankful for today? Think of as many things as possible, no matter how big or small they are.
3. Do you feel any differently about your worries after writing your gratitude list? If so, explain how you feel.

CHAPTER EIGHT

Perfect Peace

When sailors describe a storm that no boat can escape, they call it a perfect storm. Hurricane-force winds, a cold front, a downpour of rain, mountain-sized waves. All the elements combine to create disaster.

But you don't need to be a fisherman or a sailor to experience a perfect storm. All you need is a bully *plus* a friend moving away. A difficult class *plus* a sickness that keeps you out of school for a week. A parent's job loss *plus* a divorce. We can handle one challenge . . . but two or three at a time? One wave after another? It's like forceful winds followed by thunderstorms. It's enough to make you wonder, *Will I survive?*

Our friend Paul offered an answer to this question in

Philippians 4:7: "And God's peace, which is so great we cannot understand it, will keep your hearts and minds in Christ Jesus."

As we do our part (be joyful, be kind and gentle, pray about everything, and practice gratitude), God does His part. He gives us His peace.

What do you think of when you hear the word *peace*? Have you felt it before? Peace is a calm feeling. Maybe you feel peace when you go on a walk outside or when you look up at a sky full of stars or when you're reading a book. Peace slows us down. It helps us breathe deeper. Peace is the sense that everything is going to be okay.

Notice that Paul said we get the peace *of* God, not peace *from* God.

God downloads the calm of His throne room into the world. We should be worried, but we aren't. We should be upset, but we are comforted. The peace of God goes beyond our understanding and the facts of our circumstances.

Have you ever felt peace when you shouldn't have? Maybe you were really nervous about something. Then you prayed about it, and all of a sudden, you felt better. The thing you were nervous about didn't go away, but you felt better in the middle of it. You felt peace.

That is God's peace.

Jesus said it this way in John 14:27: "I leave you peace; my peace I give you. I do not give it to you as the world does. So don't let your hearts be troubled or afraid."

A Real Perfect Storm

Paul said this peace will keep our hearts and minds in Christ Jesus. The New King James Version of Philippians 4:7 says that this peace will *guard* our hearts and minds. God protects our hearts and minds when we believe in Him.

Paul believed God protected him, and he had proof.

Paul often went on long journeys to spread the gospel. During one of these trips, he rode on a ship across the Mediterranean Sea. (You can read the whole story in Acts 27:1–12.) This ship was big, sturdy, and strong, but it wasn't built to sail through big waves and winds. Paul warned the sailors that they shouldn't go the route they wanted to take. It was wintertime, and Paul knew that particular path was really cold and cloudy during the winter. The cold air would make the waves and wind extra strong. And the cloudy skies would make it difficult to see.

But the sailors took that route anyway.

And soon a great wind came up. The temperature dropped. The sails whipped. The waves frothed. The sailors searched for land and couldn't see it. They looked at the storm and couldn't avoid it.

The pieces of the perfect storm were gathering:

1. a winter sea
2. a ferocious wind
3. a clumsy boat
4. an impatient crew

Individually, these elements were manageable. But all together they were terrifying.

The storm lasted for fourteen days (verse 27)! Fourteen hours would shake you. (Fourteen minutes would undo me!) But two weeks of sunless days and starless nights? Fourteen days of bouncing, climbing toward the heavens and plunging toward the sea. The ocean boomed, splashed, and rumbled. The sailors lost all appetite for food. They lost all reason for hope. They gave up. And when they gave up, Paul spoke up:

> Men, you should have listened to me. You should not have sailed from Crete. Then you would not have all this trouble and loss. But now I tell you to cheer up because none of you will die. Only the ship will be lost. Last night an angel came to me from the God I belong to and worship. The angel said, "Paul, do not be afraid. You must stand before Caesar. And God has promised you that he will save the lives of everyone sailing with you." So men, have courage. I trust in God that everything will happen as his angel told me.
>
> —Acts 27:21–25

Paul wasn't a sailor or a captain, but the sailors listened to him. Why? Because Paul gave them a reason to hope.

Maybe you need Paul's words today in whatever storm you are going through: *cheer up . . . do not be afraid . . . have courage . . . trust in God.* These words can bring us peace during our own perfect storms.

Ways to Feel CALM

Breathe
When you feel anxious, take five slow, deep breaths.

Exercise
Moving your body produces a chemical in your brain that makes you feel happy.

Talk
Tell someone how you feel. Share your worries with a friend, parent, teacher, pastor, or therapist.

Eat Healthy
Your mind works best when your body is fed with good things.

Pray
Tell God how you're feeling, and ask Him for help. Trust Him to take care of your worry.

Journal
Put your worries into words, and they will feel smaller.

Rest
Your mind needs rest as much as your body does. Get enough sleep and spend time doing things that make you feel calm.

"You Should Have Listened"

Paul told the sailors, "Men, you should have listened to me" (verse 21). If they had, they wouldn't have gotten into such a crazy storm.

This can happen with God's instructions too. When we don't listen to God, we can find ourselves in a mess.

You might be wondering, *How do I know what God is saying to me?*

God doesn't usually yell down at us from the sky. At least, that hasn't been my experience. But God does talk to us. He talks to us through His Word, prayer, and other people.

> **God's Word:** The Bible tells us what God thinks about a lot of different things, like how we should treat others and love others.
>
> **Prayer:** God can speak to us when we pray. It probably won't sound like an actual voice, but it might be a feeling in your heart or a thought that doesn't come from you.
>
> **Others:** Sometimes other people give us good advice or loving words. God uses others to tell us the things He wants us to hear.

When we don't listen to God through the Bible, prayer, or people we trust, we can get into unnecessary trouble.

For example, maybe you learned at church that you should respect your parents. You know this is an important thing to do, but you don't always do it. The other day, your mom told you to put your phone away during dinner when you were messaging a friend. But you kept texting.

Because you disobeyed, your mom took your phone for the rest of the night.

If you had respected your mom in the first place, you could have checked your phone after dinner. Now, you can't check it until tomorrow morning, and you're worried about what you'll miss.

If you've ever done something like this, don't worry. It doesn't mean you're a bad person or a bad Christian. Take a moment to remember what God told you in the first place. And remember that He still loves you just as much as He ever has. He will give you a second chance. In fact, with God, we have more than second chances. We have third, fourth, fifth, and hundredth chances!

An Angel Came

Paul scolded the sailors for disregarding his good advice. But he also gave them two promises.

The first promise was that heaven sends angels to help us.

Paul told the sailors, "Last night an angel came to me" (verse 23). On the deck of a sinking ship in a raging storm, Paul received a visitor from heaven. An angel came and stood beside him.

Angels still come and help us.

Yesterday Oliver posted a video of his cat, Murray. Usually people make nice or funny comments on videos of Murray. But this time, a guy from school made fun of Oliver for being a "cat guy." Oliver wanted to write something mean back, but he remembered something Jesus said in the Bible: "You have heard that it was said, 'An eye for an eye, and a tooth for a tooth.' But I tell you, don't stand up against an evil person. If someone slaps you on the right cheek, turn to him the other cheek also" (Matthew 5:38–39).

Oliver knew this meant that Christians aren't supposed to get people back. He was about to turn off the computer, but then he saw that other people had liked the guy's comment. Oliver got so mad that he ended up writing something mean back after all. He and the other guy went back and forth saying mean things to each other. Oliver went to sleep that night feeling ashamed of the mean things he said to the bully. He also felt ashamed about the mean things the bully said to him.

Have you ever known you shouldn't say or do something, but you said or did it anyway? How did that make you feel? What should Oliver have done in this situation?

One Sunday morning after I preached at church, one of our members came up to me and said, "I saw your angel."

"You did?" I asked her.

"Yes, he stood near you as you preached."

I find comfort in that thought, and I believe it because several passages of Scripture talk about angels. Hebrews 1:14 says, "All the angels are spirits who serve God and are sent to help those who will receive salvation."

There are lots of stories of angels visiting people in the Bible. In Daniel 10:4–14, an angel gave Daniel a message about the future. And an angel protected Shadrach, Meshach, and Abednego from fire in Daniel 3:16–28. In Luke 1:26–38, an angel told Mary that she was going to be the mother of God's Son. An angel also visited Joseph, Jesus' earthly dad, in Matthew 1:18–25. And an angel was with Peter in prison in Acts 12:3–19.

Psalm 91:11 says, "[God] has put his angels in charge of you to watch over you wherever you go."

If God sent His angels to people in the Bible, we can be sure He is still sending them to us today. They protect us and are with us, even in our storms.

You Belong to God

The second promise we can find in the story of Paul's storm is that heaven has a place for us.

Paul knew this. He said, "Last night an angel came to me from the God I belong to" (Acts 27:23).

When kids go to summer camp, parents have to sign a form that names the person responsible for the child. If you break a leg or get sick, the camp needs to know who to call to take care of you. Hopefully your mom or dad signs their name on that form!

God signed His name for you.

When you gave your life to Him, He took responsibility for you. He will make sure you always make it home safely because you are His.

You are His sheep; He is your shepherd. Jesus said, "I am the good shepherd. I know my sheep, and my sheep know me" (John 10:14).

You are His child; He is your father. "So now you are not a slave; you are God's child, and God will give you the blessing he promised, because you are his child" (Galatians 4:7).

You can have peace in the midst of the storm because you are not alone. You belong to God. God has never promised a life with no storms. But He has promised to be there when you face them.

God Fights for You

A king named Jehoshaphat (jeh-ho-suh-fat) in the Old Testament trusted God to be with him when his enemies gathered for a war.

The Moabites were a powerful nation located near Israel. They gathered a bunch of other nations together to fight against the Israelites. It was a military version of a perfect storm. Israel could handle one army at a time, but not all these armies at once.

But Jehoshaphat knew what to do. He didn't add men to his army or build more weapons. He turned to God. Jehoshaphat prayed, "We have no power. . . . We don't know what to do, so we look to you for help" (2 Chronicles 20:12).

God responded with this message: "Don't be afraid or discouraged because of this large army. The battle is not your battle, it is God's" (verse 15).

Jehoshaphat so totally believed in God that he decided to march into battle with singers leading the army (verse 21). These singers sang worship songs to God. Jehoshaphat knew the real battle was a spiritual one, so he started with worship.

By the time the Israelites reached the battlefield, the war was over. The enemies had turned on each other (verses 22–24).

Learn a lesson from King Jehoshaphat. Start with worship. Go first to your Father in prayer and praise. Confess to Him your fears. Gather with His people. Expect to see Mighty God fight for you. He is near, as near as your next breath.

Jesus Will Catch You

A boy named Noah Drew was only two years old when he learned that God is near. The Drew family was making the short drive from their house to their neighborhood pool. Leigh Anna, Noah's mom, didn't realize the car doors weren't locked. As Leigh Anna drove, Noah opened his door and fell out.

Leigh Anna felt a bump, like she had driven over a speed bump, and stopped the car. Her husband, Ben, jumped out and found Noah on the street. It hadn't been a speed bump. She had hit Noah.

"He's alive!" Ben shouted. Noah's legs were covered in blood, and he was shaking. Leigh Anna hurried over to the passenger seat and held Noah on her lap as Ben drove to the hospital.

After getting an X-ray, the doctors said Noah had no broken bones! A five-thousand-pound vehicle had run over his legs, but little Noah had nothing but cuts and bruises. It was a miracle.

Later that night Leigh Anna dropped to her knees and thanked Jesus for saving her son. She lay down next to Noah. She thought Noah was asleep. But as she lay beside him in the dark, he said, "Mama, Jesus catched me."

She said, "He did?"

Noah replied, "I told Jesus thank You, and He said you're very welcome."

The next day Noah said, "Mama, Jesus has brown hands. He catched me like this." He held his arms out, cupping his little hands. The next day he told her that Jesus has brown hair. When she asked him for more information, he said, "That's all." But when he said his prayers that night, he said, "Thank You, Jesus, for catching me."

Perfect storms bear down on the best of us. Shoving winds. Crashing waves. They come. But Jesus still catches His children. He still holds out His arms. He still sends His angels. Because you belong to Him, you can have peace in the midst of the storm. The same Jesus who sent the angel to Paul sends this message to you: "When you pass through the waters, I will be with you" (Isaiah 43:2).

You may be facing the perfect storm. But Jesus offers the perfect peace.

Brain & Heart Check

1. Have you ever been in a bad situation because you didn't listen to God? What happened? What were God's instructions?
2. Look back at "Ways to Feel Calm" earlier in the chapter. Choose one tool to try this week.
3. Do you have a storm that you need God's help with right now? Tell Him about it, and tell Him exactly what you need. Then thank Him for being with you in the middle of your trouble.

SECTION 4

Think About Good Things

**Think about the things that are
good and worthy of praise.**
—Philippians 4:8

CHAPTER NINE

Think About What You Think About

When Rebecca Taylor was just thirteen years old, she had already had more than fifty-five surgeries. She had spent about one thousand days in the hospital. Rebecca has a disease called pancreatitis that has caused her to feel sick for most of her life so far.

Rebecca's mom, Christyn, has a blog about Rebecca and her health to keep all of her friends and family updated. In one post she wrote about how Rebecca's doctors told her that because of her disease, she could have what is called a hemorrhagic stroke, which is when your brain starts to bleed. If Rebecca had one of these strokes, she could become even more sick.

Those words *hemorrhagic stroke* really scared Christyn, but she was able to find peace in the middle of the storm. Read what she wrote in this blog post:

This past week's new land mine was the phrase "possible hemorrhagic stroke," a phrase I heard dozens of times used by numerous physicians. Over and over and over that phrase filled my mind and consumed my thoughts. It was emotionally crippling.

This past Sunday our preacher, Max Lucado, started a very fitting series on anxiety. We reviewed the familiar Philippians 4:6 verse: "Do not be anxious about anything, but in everything, by prayer and petition, with thanksgiving, present your requests to God."

I presented my requests to the Lord as I had so many times before, but this time, THIS time, I needed more. And so, using Philippians 4:8–9 [NIV, 1985] as a guide, I found my answer:

"Finally, brothers, whatever is true . . ." What was true in my life at this particular moment? The blessing of all family members eating dinner together.

"Whatever is noble." The blessing of enjoying each other's presence outside of a hospital room.

"Whatever is right." The blessing of experiencing my two sons' daily lives.

"Whatever is pure." The blessing of all three children laughing and playing with each other.

"Whatever is lovely." The blessing of watching Rebecca sleep peacefully in her bed at night.

"Whatever is admirable." The blessing of an honorable team working tirelessly on Rebecca's care.

"If anything is excellent." The blessing of watching a miracle unfold.

"Or praiseworthy." The blessing of worshipping a Lord who is worthy to be praised.

"Think about such things."

I did. As I meditated on these things, I stopped the dreaded phrase "hemorrhagic stroke" from sucking any joy out of my life. . . . And when I dwelt on the bountiful blessings in my life happening AT THAT VERY MOMENT, "the peace of God, which transcends all understanding," DID guard my heart and my mind in Christ Jesus. A true, unexpected miracle. Thank You, Lord.

Did you see what Christyn did? The words *hemorrhagic stroke* hovered over her life like a thundercloud. Yet she stopped the awful phrase from sucking joy out of her life by following Paul's teaching in Philippians 4: "Think about the things that are true and honorable and right and pure and beautiful and respected" (verse 8).

Another translation of this verse says to "meditate on these things" (NKJV).

Meditate means to think about something with your full attention. So Paul was telling us to completely focus on the good things. Give zero attention to the mishaps, the struggles, and the disappointments. Because how we think affects how we feel and act.

Rebecca's mom was able to control her fear by controlling her thoughts. She focused on the positive instead of the negative. She picked what she pondered. You can do this too!

CHOOSE HAPPY THOUGHTS

1. Write in a gratitude journal.
2. Memorize Bible verses.
3. Sing or listen to worship songs.
4. Spend time with encouraging people.
5. Write positive comments on your friends' social media posts.
6. Say "thank you" to someone.
7. Take a nature walk.
8. Do a favor for someone.
9. Tell someone how much they mean to you.
10. Give yourself a compliment.

Air Traffic Control

You didn't select your birthplace or birth date. You didn't choose your parents or siblings. You don't determine the weather or the amount of salt in the ocean. There are many things in life you have no choice about. But the greatest decision of life is within your ability. You can choose what you think about.

You can be the air traffic controller of the airport of

your mind. You are in the control tower and can direct the thought traffic of your world. Thoughts circle above, coming and going. If

Thoughts have consequences.

one of them lands, it is because you gave it permission. If it leaves, it is because you directed it to go away. You can select your thought pattern.

Proverbs 4:23 says, "Be careful what you think, because your thoughts run your life." Do you want to feel happy tomorrow? Then think happy thoughts today. Do you want to guarantee tomorrow's misery? Then let yourself drown in the mud of self-pity or guilt or anxiety today. Thoughts have consequences.

People who think more positive thoughts live longer.

People who exercise regularly have more energy.

People who exercise feel sad, low, anxious, or depressed half as often.

A positive attitude strengthens your body to better fight illness.

Truth Triumphs

Healing from anxiety means you must think in a healthy way. The hard thing you are facing isn't making you feel anxious. Your thoughts about that hard thing are making you anxious. Think about that!

Satan knows this about us. The Bible describes the Devil as the "father of lies" (John 8:44). He comes to kill, steal, and destroy (John 10:10). He is an evil spirit that tempts us, makes us feel bad about ourselves, and tells us lies. God is love, but the Devil is hate. The Devil is especially good at putting negative and anxious thoughts in our heads and convincing us that these lies are true.

I don't say this to freak you out. You need to be aware that there is a force of evil out there so you can protect yourself from it. Remember, you are the air traffic controller of your mind. When thoughts from the Devil circle, send them away. And invite new, positive, true thoughts to land.

Anytime you begin thinking negative thoughts, fight back with the kinds of thoughts Paul listed in Philippians 4:8—thoughts that are true, honorable, right, pure, beautiful, and respected.

Now I See

When I was in fifth grade, I didn't know I needed glasses. I assumed my classmates saw what I saw when they looked at the blackboard: a patch of fuzzy lines. I didn't ask them if they could see the baseball when it left the pitcher's hand or the football when the kicker kicked it. I assumed they saw the ball when I did, at the last minute, with barely enough time to swing the bat or make the catch.

I had poor vision. But I didn't know it. I had never known anything else.

FIGHT LIES WITH GOD'S TRUTH

When the Devil tells you . . .		Remember God says. . .
No one will ever love me.	⟹	God loves me (Romans 8:38–39).
I'm a terrible person.	⟹	In Christ, I am forgiven (Ephesians 4:32).
I don't have any friends.	⟹	I have a friend in Jesus (John 15:15).
Everyone hates me.	⟹	No matter how others feel about me, I can love them. (Matthew 5:44)
I'll never do well in school.	⟹	I can do all things with Christ's strength (Philippians 4:13)

Then my teacher called my mom. My mom called the eye doctor. The eye doctor asked me to read some letters on a chart. The next thing I knew, I was handed my first pair of glasses. Talk about a game changer! From one moment to the next, the fuzzy lines became clear. The baseball became big. The football was catchable.

I still remember the thrill of sudden sight. I would sit in Mrs. Collins's fifth grade classroom and lift and lower my glasses, moving from blurry to twenty-twenty vision, from unclear images to sharp faces. Suddenly I could see.

Christians, too, talk about the joy of sudden sight. We love to sing the old hymn: "Amazing grace! How sweet the sound that saved a wretch like me! I once was lost, but now I am found; was blind, but now I see." Blind. Unable to see God's love. Unable to see the truth of salvation in Jesus. But then Jesus restores our sight.

People who don't know Jesus simply cannot see clearly. "The devil who rules this world has blinded the minds of those who do not believe. They cannot see the light of the Good News—the Good News about the glory of Christ, who is exactly like God" (2 Corinthians 4:4). We need a spiritual eye doctor. We need Jesus to do for us what He did for the man on the side of the Jerusalem road.

As Jesus was walking along, He saw a man who had been born blind (John 9:1). No one else saw him. The followers of Jesus may have observed the blind man. But they did not *see* him.

The disciples only saw a spiritual puzzle. Jesus' followers

Emma was looking at social media on the way to school. She saw a post about her friend's birthday party the next weekend. Emma didn't know her friend was having a birthday party. Emma hadn't been invited. As her dad drove, she got more and more upset. She had thoughts like:

My friend doesn't like me anymore.
I bet she invited everybody but me.
None of my friends like me.
I never get invited to anything.
I'll be alone all weekend.

When Emma got out of her dad's car, her friend ran up to her. "Emma!" she said. "Why haven't you responded to my DM?"

"What DM?" Emma asked.

"I sent it this morning. About my party. Can you come?"

Emma checked her DMs. There was an invite to her friend's birthday party. Emma had missed the message because she was so worried about not being invited.

What could Emma have done differently after she saw the post? What are some true, positive thoughts that could have replaced her negative thoughts?

asked Him, "Teacher, whose sin caused this man to be born blind—his own sin or his parents' sin?" (verse 2). They didn't see a human being; they saw a topic of discussion.

Jesus, by contrast, saw a man who was blind from birth, a man who'd never seen a sunrise, who couldn't distinguish purple from pink. A man who dwelled in a dark world.

Jesus *saw* him. In John 9:3–7, He answered:

> "It is not this man's sin or his parents' sin that made him blind. This man was born blind so that God's power could be shown in him. While it is daytime, we must continue doing the work of the One who sent me. Night is coming, when no one can work. While I am in the world, I am the light of the world."
>
> After Jesus said this, he spit on the ground and made some mud with it and put the mud on the man's eyes. Then he told the man, "Go and wash in the Pool of Siloam." (Siloam means Sent.) So the man went, washed, and came back seeing.

Nothing has changed. Jesus still finds blind people and restores their sight. He promised that through His ministry "the blind . . . can see" (Luke 4:18). He came to give light and sight.

Jesus wants to help you see clearly. Our own perspective, especially when we are anxious, is not always the true perspective. Jesus can help you see for yourself who you really are: His child, loved by Him. He helps you see that you are forgiven when you feel anxious about a mistake you made. He helps you see beauty in the middle of a bad day. When Jesus helps us see, we start to see things in a new way.

Remember our friend Rebecca? Right before her thirteenth birthday, she went back for a doctor's visit. Seven months earlier Rebecca was barely surviving. Now, Rebecca was full of life. She had gained thirty pounds. Her health was improving. Her doctors called her a "walking miracle."

Her mom, Christyn, wrote on her blog: "I watched these interactions with a silent sense of awe. It is easy to praise God during seasons of wellness. But it was during my greatest distress when I felt the Lord's presence poured upon me. And it was in those heart- 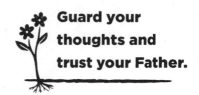 breaking moments I learned to trust this God who provided unimaginable strength during unimaginable pain."

God will help you too. Guard your thoughts and trust your Father.

Brain & Heart Check

1. Write down the thoughts you had yesterday. What thoughts did you have about yourself? How did you feel about others? How did you feel about what happened during the day?

2. What kind of thoughts are these? Label each one as a truth or lie and positive or negative.

3. Go through each untrue or negative thought in your list. Replace it with something true, honorable, right, pure, beautiful, or respected.

CHAPTER TEN

Cling to Christ

—————————————

Are you trying to follow God, but it just seems like a *struggle?* So many things to do. So many things to *not* do. You worry about messing up, but sometimes you're tired of trying *so hard.*

The answer has to do with grapes.

Yep, grapes. Stay with me, and you'll see what I mean.

There was a farmer who had a vineyard of grapes. One day he noticed his vines weren't growing. Leaves drooped. Vines dragged.

The farmer went out to his vineyard to see what was going on. He set a stool between the rows, pulled off his hat, and asked, "Okay, guys. Why the gloom?"

At first none of the branches spoke. Finally, one branch opened up, "I just can't do it anymore!" he blurted. "I squeeze and I push, but the grapes won't come."

Leaves bounced as other branches nodded in agreement. "I can't even get a raisin to pop out," one confessed.

"I'm so tired," offered one more.

The farmer shook his head and sighed. "No wonder you guys are unhappy. You're trying to do what you can't do. And you're forgetting to do what you were made to do. Stop trying to force the fruit. Your job is to hang on to the vine. Get a grip! You'll be amazed by what you will produce."

Sound ridiculous? We know that crops can't talk to farmers, but if you will not roll your eyes *too* hard at this silly story, you'll learn something critical to overcoming anxiety. You see, the farmer's conversation with his plants is similar to the conversation God wants to have with us.

No, God doesn't want to chat about grapes. But He does want to talk about fruit. Spiritual fruit.

Spiritual fruit is anything good that grows out of us when Jesus is in our hearts—things like love, joy, peace, patience, kindness, goodness, faithfulness, gentleness, and self-control (Galatians 5:22–23).

We can try to be peaceful. We can try to be patient. We can try to be kind and good and faithful and gentle and self-controlled. But it's hard sometimes, isn't it?

Maybe you felt this way when you tried to meditate on good things. All day you tried to think about only what was good, true, honorable, and respectful. But you caught your mind wandering. You thought negative things about yourself and others. You imagined worst-case scenarios. You lost sight of the truth you know from Scripture.

When we try to be good, it's easy to feel like we've failed. Because on our own, it's really hard to be good.

But I have good news for you! We don't have to try so hard.

Think about the farmer's branches. They were putting a lot

We don't have to try so hard.

of pressure on themselves to do a job they were never meant to do. Their job was not to grow grapes. Their job was simple: hold on to the vine. Then, the fruit would come.

Our Vine

It's the same with us and our spiritual fruit. It's not our job to make ourselves more spiritual. We just have to hold on to Jesus.

Jesus explained this in John 15:4–10:

> "Remain in me, and I will remain in you. A branch cannot produce fruit alone but must remain in the vine. In the same way, you cannot produce fruit alone but must remain in me.
>
> I am the vine, and you are the branches. If any remain in me and I remain in them, they produce much fruit. But without me they can do nothing. If any do not remain in me, they are like a branch that is thrown away and then dies. People pick up dead branches, throw

them into the fire, and burn them. If you remain in me and follow my teachings, you can ask anything you want, and it will be given to you. You should produce much fruit and show that you are my followers, which brings glory to my Father. I loved you as the Father loved me. Now remain in my love. I have obeyed my Father's commands, and I remain in his love. In the same way, if you obey my commands, you will remain in my love."

Jesus made three comparisons in this passage:

God is like a farmer. A farmer loves to make his vines grow. He waters them, provides rich soil, and cuts away any weeds that are getting in the way. His goal is to do whatever he can to produce as many grapes as possible.

For us that means God watches over us. He gives us what we need to grow: love, a solid foundation, grace, and forgiveness.

Jesus is like a vine. The vine is rooted in the soil. Branches grow out of the vine, but the vine is sturdier than its branches. It is a strong root for the branches to hold on to. The vine carries nutrients from the soil into the branches.

For us this means Jesus holds us in place. He keeps us safe and secure. He gives us the nutrients we need to feel peaceful, be gentle, and think about good things.

We are like branches. We can only grow when we're firmly attached to the vine—Jesus. Jesus gives us everything we need so we don't have to produce it ourselves. All we have to do is grip tightly on to Him. We hold on to Jesus by remembering who He is, praying, worshipping Him, and reading His words in Scripture. When we do this, we grow the fruit of love, joy, peace, patience, kindness, goodness, faithfulness, gentleness, and self-control.

Scripture says that when we remain in Jesus, we will bring glory to God (John 15:8). This is because when we are peaceful, others notice. When we are gentle, others see it. When we are kind, others are blessed. They wonder how we're able to bear so much spiritual fruit in our lives. And we tell them, "It's not me. It's Jesus. I simply remain in Him."

This is why our fruit matters to God, and it should matter to you. If you want to be anxious for nothing, this is how you do it. Not by trying harder but by holding on tighter to Jesus. Our assignment is not fruitfulness but faithfulness.

Our Home

Another translation of John 15:4–10 uses the word *abide* instead of *remain*. *Abide* means to live. Wherever you abide is where you live. Underline this word anytime you see it in the passage:

> Abide in Me, and I in you. As the branch cannot bear fruit of itself unless it abides in the vine, so neither can you unless you abide in Me. . . . He who abides in Me and I in him, he bears much fruit. . . . If anyone does not abide in Me, he is thrown away as a branch and dries up. . . . If you abide in Me, and My words abide in you, ask whatever you wish, and it will be done for you. . . . Abide in My love. . . . Abide in My love; just as I have kept My Father's commandments and abide in His love (NASB).

"Come, live in Me!" Jesus invites. "Make My home your home."

Home is safe. There, you can escape from bullies and hard classes. Home is comfortable. It's where you can be yourself. You can wear your pajamas, listen to your favorite music, and relax. Home is familiar. You know right where everything is; home is your space.

Jesus wants us to make our home in Him. He is our safe place. We are comfortable in His presence and free to be ourselves. He knows His way around our hearts. We can rest in Him. His roof of grace protects us from storms of guilt. His walls of wisdom keep us safe from confusion and anxiety. Jesus is the safest, warmest, most comfortable home we could ever have.

ways to Hold on to Jesus

Read the Bible.

Sing worship songs.

Write in a prayer or gratitude journal.

Take a walk and notice all the things God made.

Pray with others.

Make a list of questions for Jesus. Look for the answers in your Bible or ask an adult for help.

Ask God for forgiveness.

Draw, paint, or make a craft for Jesus.

Memorize a Bible verse.

Hold On

If we abide in Christ, we never let go of Him, just like the branch never lets go of the vine. Our main job is to keep holding on to Jesus.

You may hear Christians say things like "We are going to make a difference for Jesus." Or "We are going to lead people to the Lord." Or "We are going to change the world!" These are all great things to say, but they are only possible when we do our first job: hold on to Jesus, hold on to the vine.

When a father leads his four-year-old son down a crowded street, he takes him by the hand and says, "Hold on to me." He doesn't say, "Memorize the map" or "Take your chances dodging the traffic" or "Let's see if you can find your way home." The good father gives the child one responsibility: "Hold on to my hand."

God does the same with us. Don't give yourself a list of "shoulds" and "shouldn'ts":

I should be kinder.
I shouldn't feel so worried all the time.
I shouldn't be so grumpy all the time.
I should share my faith with my friends more.

Don't worry about all the things you should be doing. Just hold Jesus' hand, and let Him take care of the rest.

Most days, Oliver looks at his phone when he wakes up and just before he goes to sleep. He checks his text messages first thing in the morning. And he checks his DMs the last thing at night.

Oliver wants to be more patient and kind on social media. He doesn't want to argue with people so much. But the more time he spends on social media, the less patient and the more judgmental he becomes.

So Oliver made a big decision. He would stop look-ing at social media right before bed. Instead, he would spend those minutes reading his Bible, listening to worship music, or journaling.

It was hard at first. As he lay in bed reading or writing, he heard alerts on his phone. Then he would get sucked into checking text messages or social media and forget all about his Bible and journal.

After a few days, Oliver decided to leave his phone outside his room at night. That way, he wouldn't see or hear his notifications. Then it would be easier to keep reading, journaling, or listening to music before bed.

How do you think this new routine made Oliver feel? What do you think about the idea of not looking at your phone before bed and spending time with God instead?

A Miracle in Africa

A missionary named Kent Brantly held on to Jesus during the scariest time of his life. Kent was a doctor working in a country in Africa called Liberia when the Ebola virus broke out. Ebola is a very deadly disease, and it was spreading quickly where Kent lived. Thousands of people had already died from it. If you got Ebola, you had a higher chance of dying than living.

Kent was treating patients who had Ebola. He had to wear a full-body suit to protect himself. He could get Ebola from simply touching one of his patients.

One day, Kent started getting the symptoms of the Ebola virus. He had a fever and a really bad stomachache. He knew he might have the virus, so he got tested. Then he waited for the results at home. His wife and kids were visiting family in the United States, so he was alone.

While he waited, he held on to Jesus by reading Scripture. He opened his Bible to the book of Hebrews and started reading. He meditated on Hebrews 4:16: "Let us, then, feel very sure that we can come before God's throne where there is grace. There we can receive mercy and grace to help us when we need it." Kent's Bible version used the phrase "with confidence" to describe how we should come to God's throne. Kent copied the scripture into his prayer journal and wrote the words "with confidence" in italics.

He closed his journal and began the wait. The next

three days were painful from the sickness and from waiting. Then the test results came back: he had Ebola.

He called his wife, Amber, who was at her parents' house in Texas. She hurried to the bedroom so they could talk in private. Kent told her, "The test results came back. It's positive."

She began to cry. They only talked for a short time before Kent was tired and had to hang up.

Amber went outside and walked across a field toward a large mesquite tree. She sat on one of its branches that was low to the ground. She wanted to pray but couldn't find the words. So she started singing an old hymn she learned when she was young. The lyrics go like this:

> *There is no shadow of turning with Thee;*
> *Thou changest not, Thy compassions, they fail not*
> *As Thou hast been Thou forever wilt be.*

The song made her feel better, so she began to sing another hymn she loved:

> *I need Thee every hour, in joy or pain;*
> *Come quickly and abide, or life is vain.*
> *I need Thee, oh I need Thee;*
> *Every hour I need Thee;*
> *Oh, bless me now, my Savior,*
> *I come to Thee.*

"I thought my husband was going to die," she wrote later in a book. "I was in pain. I was afraid. Through those hymns, though, I was able to connect with God in a meaningful way when I couldn't find my own words to pray."

Kent was able to fly from Liberia to Atlanta, Georgia, to go to a hospital there. After a few days, he started to feel better. His story was on the news. Everybody knew about Kent. They knew he might die. And they all rejoiced when he got better and was able to leave the hospital.

Kent and Amber could have let anxiety take over. But instead they held on to Jesus. They meditated on Scripture and hymns. They filled their minds with the truth of God, and God calmed their hearts.

Look

Jesus is there for us like He was there for Kent and Amber. He told us in the Bible, "Don't worry about the food or drink you need to live, or about the clothes you need for your body" (Matthew 6:25).

Then He told us to do one thing: look. He said, "Look at the birds in the air. They don't plant or harvest or store food in barns, but your heavenly Father feeds them. And you know that you are worth much more than the birds. You cannot add any time to your life by worrying about it" (verses 26–27). The birds depend on God. They trust Him to give them everything they need.

Finally, Jesus told us to look at the lilies of the field. "And why do you worry about clothes? Look at how the lilies in the field grow. They don't work or make clothes for themselves. But I tell you that even Solomon with his riches was not dressed as beautifully as one of these flowers" (verses 28–29).

If God cares about birds and flowers, you can be certain He cares about you too. Next time you start to feel worried, look. Look at the birds. Look at the flowers. God takes care of them. He will take care of you.

HOW TO GET HELP WITH ANXIETY

Talk to your school counselor or social worker.

Ask your parents about making an appointment with a therapist.

Talk to your youth pastor or someone you trust at church.

Call this helpline: 1-800-662-4357. A trained professional will listen to how you're feeling and will help you decide how to get help.

Be Set Free

My friend recently told me she drives an hour and a half to get to work each day.

"Oh, that's terrible!" I told her.

"Don't feel sorry for me," she said with a smile. "I use the trip to think about God." She told me she fills the hour and a half with worship and sermons. She listens to entire books of the Bible. She recites prayers. By the time she reaches her job, she is ready for the day.

"I turn my commute into my chapel," she said.

Can you do this? Do you have time in your day you could spend with God? Maybe you could put down your phone for a few minutes and open your Bible. Set your alarm ten minutes earlier in the morning and spend time in prayer before school. Or instead of watching TV at night, listen to an audio version of a Christian book or book of the Bible.

Jesus said, "If you abide in my word, you are truly my disciples, and you will know the truth, and the truth will set you free" (John 8:31–32 ESV). When we abide in Jesus, who is the Truth, and when we hold on to Him like a branch holds on to the vine, we are free. Free from fear. And free from anxiety.

Brain & Heart Check

1. Think about all the meanings of the word *home*. Take pictures to make a photo collection that communicates your interpretation of *home*.

2. Write down your schedule for today. Start with when you woke up. Include school, activities, homework, chores, and anything else you did. Now underline or highlight the times you were spending time with Jesus. Do you need to make more room for Jesus to live with you? At what time of day could you set aside fifteen minutes to spend with Him?

CHAPTER ELEVEN

C.A.L.M.

It's the night before your first day at a new school. You can't fall asleep. You keep checking your phone. You scroll through social media, hoping it will get your mind off tomorrow. But instead, you keep seeing your friends from your old school post about how excited they are to go back to school.

You're not excited. You're nervous. You're nervous about being the new kid. You're worried the haircut your mom made you get doesn't look good. You're worried you won't make any friends, you won't be able to find your classrooms, and you'll have no one to sit with at lunch.

You turn off your phone. It's not helping you feel any better. But as you close your eyes, the questions keep coming. *What if I miss the bus? What if I bring the wrong gym clothes? What if everyone thinks I'm weird? What if, what if, what if. . . ?*

What does all of this fear and anxiety mean?

It means you're human.

Feeling anxious about a new school—or a new year, a new sports team, a new summer camp, or whatever!—doesn't mean there's something wrong with you. It doesn't mean you need to get a grip on your life and calm down. It doesn't mean you're crazy or dramatic. Being anxious just means one thing: you are human. And hear this: being anxious does not mean you're a bad Christian.

Christians have anxiety just like everybody else. Even Jesus felt anxious. On the night before His crucifixion, He was so anxious that He sweat blood (Luke 22:44). That's a real medical condition. You can look it up. He asked God to change the plan so He wouldn't have to go through the pain of the cross (Matthew 26:36–44).

But Jesus didn't stay anxious. He gave His fears to God. And with Jesus' help, we can do the same.

Let's read Paul's words one more time in Philippians 4:4–8:

> Be full of joy in the Lord always. I will say again, be full of joy.
>
> Let everyone see that you are gentle and kind. The Lord is coming soon. Do not worry about anything, but pray and ask God for everything you need, always giving

thanks. And God's peace, which is so great we cannot understand it, will keep your hearts and minds in Christ Jesus.

Brothers and sisters, think about the things that are good and worthy of praise. Think about the things that are true and honorable and right and pure and beautiful and respected.

Paul's words give us some pretty good advice about anxiety. When we do what Paul said, we can move from anxiety to peace and tranquility.

If anxiety and tranquility were trees, which one would you want to climb? The anxie-tree or the tranquili-tree? (See what I did there?)

The anxie-tree doesn't have many leaves. It has a few small branches that are so weak, the wind can whip them back and forth. It doesn't feel like a safe tree to climb because its branches are so thin. The anxie-tree is a sad tree.

The tranquili-tree, on the other hand, is a big, beautiful, strong tree. It's safe for you to climb. Its branches are big enough to sit on or even stretch out and take a nap in. It has plenty of leaves to shield you from the sun. And even when the wind blows hard, the tranquili-tree stands strong.

My guess is you'd rather climb the tranquili-tree. But how do you do that?

Begin with God.

Celebrate God's Goodness

As Paul said, "Be full of joy in the Lord always. I will say again, be full of joy" (Philippians 4:4).

Turn your attention away from your problem and focus on celebrating God. It does you no good to obsess over what you're anxious about. The more you stare at it, the bigger it grows. Yet the more you look at God, the bigger He becomes. Your problem starts to look its proper size compared to the Lord of the universe. This is what Psalm 121:1–2 (NASB) says:

> I will raise my eyes to the mountains;
> From where will my help come?
> My help comes from the LORD,
> who made heaven and earth.

Do you see the decision in those words? "I *will* raise my eyes."

Don't meditate on your mess. You gain nothing by setting your eyes on the problem. You gain everything by setting your eyes on the Lord.

Don't meditate on your mess.

This is what the disciple Peter did in that storm in the Sea of Galilee. He was a fisherman. He knew what ten-foot waves could do to small boats. Maybe that is why he volunteered to leave the craft when he saw Jesus walking on the water through the storm.

> Peter said, "Lord, if it is really you, then command me to come to you on the water."
>
> Jesus said, "Come."
>
> And Peter left the boat and walked on the water to Jesus. But when Peter saw the wind and the waves, he became afraid and began to sink. He shouted, "Lord, save me!"
>
> —Matthew 14:28–30

As long as Peter kept looking at Jesus, he could do the impossible. The moment he looked at the storm around him, he sank like a stone. If you are sinking in anxiety, it is because you are looking in the wrong direction.

Fix your eyes on the face of the One who can calm the storm.

God is sovereign. He is in control. He knows the good things He has for you. He sees your fears. He hears your prayers. He has answers for your questions.

And God is merciful. His grace is great. He has forgiven us through His Son, Jesus. Because of this, we don't have to feel guilt or shame.

Celebrate all of God's joys. This is step one. Do not hurry past this step. Face God before you face your problem. Then you will be ready to . . .

Face God before you face your problem.

C.A.L.M.

1. Celebrate God.

Be full of joy in the Lord always. I will say again, be full of joy. —Philippians 4:4

2. Ask God for help.

Pray and ask God for everything you need... —Philippians 4:6

3. Look on the bright side.

...always giving thanks. —Philippians 4:6

4. Meditate on good things.

Think about the things that are good and worthy of praise. Think about the things that are true and honorable and right and pure and beautiful and respected. —Philippians 4:8

Ask God for Help

Paul said, "Do not worry about anything, but pray and ask God for everything you need" (Philippians 4:6).

When we're afraid, we can either choose prayer or despair. Choose wisely.

You can ask God for everything you need. Not just big things but small things too. Whatever makes you feel worried, give it to God. Ask Him for help before you try to fix your problems on your own.

God said, "Call to me in times of trouble" (Psalm 50:15).

Jesus said, "Ask, and God will give to you. Search, and you will find. Knock, and the door will open for you" (Matthew 7:7). He didn't say, "Ask, and God *might* give to you. Search, and you *might* find." When we ask, He *will* listen.

Pray for every detail. God doesn't get tired of listening to us. The more details we give Him, the easier it is to know when God answers our prayers.

So ask! When anxiety knocks on the door, say "Jesus, would You mind answering that?" Let Him do what He's so good at.

Look on the Bright Side

Paul said to ask for everything we need, "always giving thanks" (Philippians 4:6).

When life feels dark and you are full of fear and anxiety, look on the bright side. Choose to have an attitude of gratitude even in the middle of hard times.

Replace anxious thoughts with grateful ones. God takes thanksgiving seriously. Why? Because gratitude keeps us focused on the present.

Have you ever noticed that when you feel really anxious, it's hard to concentrate on your homework or what someone is saying to you? This is because anxiety causes our brains to feel scattered.

We worry about the past—what we said or did. We worry about the future—tomorrow's assignments or the next decade's developments. Anxiety takes our attention from the right now and directs it "back then" or "over there."

But when you aren't focused on your problem, you suddenly have lots of room in your brain. Use it! What are you thankful for right here, right now?

Think About Good Things

Paul said, "Think about the things that are good and worthy of praise. Think about the things that are true and honorable and right and pure and beautiful and respected" (Philippians 4:8).

Don't let anxious, negative thoughts take over your mind. You can't control your circumstances, but you can control how you think about them.

One of the hardest jobs I've ever had was being a door-to-door salesman for a summer in college in Dalton, Georgia. I was nineteen years old and thousands of miles from home. I had gone with a couple of friends, but they quit after a week. I stayed.

You can't control your circumstances, but you can control how you think about them.

The job was hard. I knocked on door after door only to have them slammed in my face. I didn't have any friends. I wasn't making any money. I was miserable. One afternoon, I went to a diner to eat a hamburger. Some magnets for sale were displayed by the cash register. When I was paying my bill, one of the magnets caught my eye. It said, "When life gives you lemons, make lemonade."

When life gets sour, turn it into something sweet.

It was a cheesy phrase, but I bought the magnet anyway. I put it on the dashboard of my car and looked at it every day.

Whenever I got discouraged, I would rub my thumb over the rubber lemon and remind myself, *I can make myself miserable, or I can make myself some lemonade.*

People still slammed doors, and I still wondered what in the world I was doing so far from home. But I survived.

Life will always give us lemons. We will always have to face hard things. We will feel anxious and afraid. We will not know what to do next. But we can choose what we do with these lemons. We can either make ourselves miserable, or we can choose to meditate on good, beautiful, and true things.

May we laugh, listen, learn, and love today. And tomorrow, may we do it all over again.

A new day awaits you, my friend. A new season in which you will worry less and trust more. A season with less fear and stronger faith. Can you imagine a life in which you are anxious for nothing? God can. And with His help, you will experience it.

Brain & Heart Check

1. What do you need to do most today? Celebrate the good things about God, ask God for help, look on the bright side, or meditate on good things? How will you do that?
2. What did you learn about anxiety in your life from this book?
3. What did you learn about yourself while reading this book?
4. What did you learn about God from this book?

A Closing Note from
Max Lucado

A couple in our church asked me to help with their tenth wedding anniversary "vow renewal" ceremony in Hawaii. Being the dedicated minister I am, I had no choice but to accept their invitation to participate.

Our time on the Big Island coincided with a dramatic lava flow from Kilauea Volcano. An eight-mile river of liquid fire burned a pathway to the Pacific Ocean. We, and some other 2,500 people, couldn't resist a visit.

Driving down the "Chain of Craters Road," a sign invited us to tune into the park system's radio station. The announcer warned us to take caution, not just of the volcano but also the tidal wave. "This is tsunami territory," the voice said. "If you feel the ground shake, seek higher ground." Higher ground, in this case, was a volcano. I began to worry.

When we left the car, a sign warned us of cracking earth. On it was a drawing of a man straddling an ever-widening crevice. The caption read, "Ground can open up at any moment."

Gulp.

Then we met a park ranger. "If it were up to me, I wouldn't let people up here," he said. "There are no trails, no lights, and this lava is 1,500 to 2,000 degrees." Not all lava, I learned, is golden. Much of it is covered with a dark crust, giving it the appearance of a rock. One false step, and I could be ankle-deep in boiling rock. Still we pressed on. Like the explorers Lewis and Clark, we had to see the ocean.

The sulfur stank. The evening trail demanded flash-lights. Steam spewed out of the ocean. We ventured onto the edge of the cliff and smiled for the camera.

Great, I remember thinking. *To one side a tsunami. To the other a volcano. A step back and I'm over the edge. A seismic shift and I'm earth bait. How did I get into this?*

Have you ever wondered the same thing?

Of course you have. Your anxiety wasn't stirred by volcanoes and tsunamis but tests, heartbreaks, family drama, and social media. You aren't sidestepping lava, but you're doing your best to avoid bad grades, bad choices, and bad people. And the effort can leave you worried.

May I conclude this book with some oh-so-welcome

news? Your heavenly Father is here to help you. You don't walk this path alone. He is a good Shepherd, a good Father, and a good Friend to all who follow His lead.

By His grace you will not only survive, you will thrive! Trust in the direction of this wonderful psalm:

> Trust the LORD and do good.
> Live in the land and feed on truth.
> Enjoy serving the LORD,
> and he will give you what you want.
> Depend on the LORD;
> trust him, and he will take care of you.
> —Psalm 37:3–5

—*Max*

Sources

Introduction

Zodhiates, Spiros, ed. *Hebrew-Greek Key Word Study Bible, New International Version.* Chattanooga, TN: AMG Publishers, 1996. #3534. 2093.

Chapter 1

Julian, Kate. "What Happened to American Childhood?" *The Atlantic.* Updated April 17, 2020. https://www.theatlantic .com/magazine/archive/2020/05/childhood-in-an-anxious -age/609079/.

Clark, Taylor. "It's Not the Job Market: The Three Real Reasons Why Americans Are More Anxious Than Ever Before." *Slate.* January 31, 2011. http://www.slate.com/articles/arts /culturebox/2011/01/its_not_the_job_market.html.

Anderson, Jenny. "Even Teens Are Worried They Spend Too Much Time on Their Phones." *Quartz.* August 23, 2018. https://qz.com/1367506/pew-research-teens-worried-they -spend-too-much-time-on-phones.

Twenge, Jean M. "Have Smartphones Destroyed a Generation?" *The Atlantic*. September 2017. https://www.theatlantic.com /magazine/archive/2017/09/has-the-smartphone-destroyed-a -generation/534198/.

McCarthy, Claire. "Anxiety in Teens Is Rising: What's Going On?" *HealthyChildren.org*. November 20, 2019. https://www .healthychildren.org/English/health-issues/conditions /emotional-problems/Pages/Anxiety-Disorders.aspx.

Chapter 2

"What Do Kids Worry About?" *Parents Canada*. May 5, 2009. https://www.parentscanada.com/school/what-do-kids-worry -about/.

Caporino, Nicole E., Shannon Exley, and Robert D. Latzman. "Youth Anxiety About Political News." *Child Psychiatry & Human Development* 51 (February 2020): 683–98. https://doi .org/10.1007/s10578-020-00972-z.

McCarthy, Claire. "Anxiety in Teens Is Rising: What's Going On?" *HealthyChildren.org*. November 20, 2019. https://www .healthychildren.org/English/health-issues/conditions /emotional-problems/Pages/Anxiety-Disorders.aspx.

Viner, Russell M., Aswathikutty Gireesh, Neza Stiglic, Lee D. Hudson, Anne-Lise Goddings, Joseph L. Ward, and Dasha E. Nicholls. "Roles of Cyberbullying, Sleep, and Physical Activity in Mediating the Effects of Social Media Use on Mental Health and Wellbeing Among Young People in England: A Secondary Analysis of Longitudinal Data." *The Lancet Child & Adolescent Health* 3, no. 10 (October 2019): 685–96. https://doi.org/10.1016/S2352 -4642(19)30186-5.

Horowitz, Juliana Menasce, and Nikki Graf. "Most U.S. Teens See Anxiety and Depression as a Major Problem Among

Their Peers." Pew Research Center. February 20, 2019. https://
www.pewsocialtrends.org/2019/02/20/most-u-s-teens-see
-anxiety-and-depression-as-a-major-problem-among-their
-peers/.

Chapter 3

Gallivan, Heather R. "Teens, Social Media and Body Image."
Park Nicollet Melrose Center. May 18, 2014. https://www
.macmh.org/wp-content/uploads/2014/05/18_Gallivan
_Teens-social-media-body-image-presentation-H-Gallivan
-Spring-2014.pdf.
Nouwen, Henri. *The Essential Henri Nouwen*. Edited by Robert
A. Jonas. Boston: Shambhala, 2009. 131–32.

Chapter 4

Smith, Melinda, Lawrence Robinson, and Jeanne Segal. "Anxiety
Disorders and Anxiety Attacks." *Help Guide*. Updated
September 2020. https://www.helpguide.org/articles/anxiety
/anxiety-disorders-and-anxiety-attacks.htm.
Common Sense Media. *Common Sense Census: Media Use by
Tweens and Teens*. November 3, 2015. https://www
.commonsensemedia.org/the-common-sense-census-media
-use-by-tweens-and-teens-infographic.
"What Social Media Does to Your Brain, According to
Neuroscience." Inverse. April 22, 2018. https://www.inverse
.com/article/43879-your-brain-on-social-media.
Moffit, Mitchell, and Gregory Brown. "5 Crazy Ways Social
Media Is Changing Your Brain Right Now." AsapSCIENCE,
September 7, 2014. Video. https://www.youtube.com/watch?v
=HffWFd_6bJ0.

Spafford, Anna T. "Telegram from Anna Spafford to Horatio Gates Spafford re Being 'Saved Alone' Among Her Traveling Party in the Shipwreck of the Ville du Havre." Library of Congress. December 2, 1873. https://www.loc.gov/item /mamcol000006.

Chapter 5

Clark, Taylor. *Nerve: Poise Under Pressure, Serenity Under Stress, and the Brave New Science of Fear and Cool.* New York: Little, Brown, 2011. 3–9.

Frey, William C. *The Dance of Hope: Finding Ourselves in the Rhythm of God's Great Story.* Colorado Springs, CO: WaterBrook Press, 2003. 175.

Chapter 6

Missions Box. "Most Americans Pray but Disagree About How Prayer Works." Press Release. August 7, 2020. https:// missionsbox.org/press-releases/most-americans-pray-but -disagree-about-how-prayer-works/.

Chapter 7

Amin, Amit. "31 Benefits of Gratitude: The Ultimate Science-Backed Guide." *Happier Human.* http://happierhuman.com /benefits-of-gratitude/.

American Psychological Association. "Growing Up Grateful Gives Teens Multiple Mental Health Benefits, New Research Shows." Press Release. August 2012. https://www.apa.org /news/press/releases/2012/08/health-benefits.

Sheldon, Kennon M., Todd B. Kashdan, and Michael F. Steger, eds. *Designing Positive Psychology: Taking Stock and Moving Forward.* New York: Oxford University Press, 2011. 249–54.

Chapter 8

Hirschlag, Ally. "Do You Live with Anxiety? Here Are 11 Ways to Cope." *Healthline.* December 17, 2018. https://www .healthline.com/health/mental-health/how-to-cope-with -anxiety#long-term-strategies.

"Tips to Manage Anxiety and Stress." *Anxiety and Depression Association of America.* https://adaa.org/tips.

Chapter 9

Danner, Deborah D., David A. Snowdon, and Wallace V. Friesen. "Positive Emotions in Early Life and Longevity: Findings from the Nun Study." *Journal of Personality and Social Psychology* 80, no. 5 (2001): 804–13. doi.org/10.1037//0022 -3514.80.5.804.

Segerstrom, Suzanne C., and Gregory E. Miller. "Psychological Stress and the Human Immune System: A Meta-Analytic Study of 30 Years of Inquiry." *Psychological Bulletin* 130, no. 4 (July 2004): 601–30. https://doi.org/10.1037/0033 -2909.130.4.601.

Sharma, Ashish, Vishal Madaan, and Frederick D. Petty. "Exercise for Mental Health." *Primary Care Companion to the Journal of Clinical Psychiatry* 8, no. 2 (2006): 106. https://doi .org/10.4088/PCC.v08n0208a.

The Lancet. "Exercise Linked to Improved Mental Health, but More May Not Always Be Better." *ScienceDaily.* August 8, 2018. https:// www.sciencedaily.com/releases/2018/08/180808193656.htm.

Chapter 10

Brantly, Kent, Amber Brantly, and David Thomas. *Called for Life: How Loving Our Neighbor Led Us into the Heart of the Ebola Epidemic.* Colorado Springs, CO: WaterBrook, 2015. 97–115.

Chisholm, Thomas Obediah, and William Marion Runyan. "Great Is Thy Faithfulness." 1923. Hope Publishing Company, 1951, Hymnal.net. https://www.hymnal.net/en/hymn/h/19.

Hawks, Annie S. "I Need Thee Every Hour." 1872. Composed by Robert Lowry. Hymnary.org. https://hymnary.org/hymn/CYBER/2967.

Resources

Websites

KidsHealth
kidshealth.org

From the nonprofit health network Nemours, KidsHealth offers doctor-reviewed articles on children's well-being, including physical health, mental health, and behavioral topics. Separate sites for kids, teens, and parents supply accurate information to help everyone learn, grow, and feel their best. From allergies and heart conditions to body image, learning disorders, and anxiety, KidsHealth provides tools to make the best health choices for your family.

Child Mind Institute
childmind.org

Parents can quickly get up to speed on the mental health and behavioral challenges facing their kids with the in-depth resources from this nonprofit dedicated to improving the lives of children and families battling mental health and learning disorders. Short articles on targeted topics provide details on symptoms, current research, and treatment options. Parent guides outline proven strategies for helping kids thrive.

Comforting Anxious Children
comfortinganxiouschildren.com

Special education teacher, mom, and anxiety warrior Janis Gioia offers articles and resources to help families calm and comfort kids with anxiety. She addresses the whole child, offering tips to soothe and strengthen mind, body, and spirit. As a mom of anxious kids, Jan walks alongside parents as they seek the best for their children. The site includes prayer tools, advice for Christian parents, and lots of hands-on practical strategies.

Books for Kids

What to Do When You Worry Too Much: A Kid's Guide to Overcoming Anxiety by Dawn Huebner (Magination Press, 2005)
The Worry Workbook for Kids: Helping Children to Overcome Anxiety and the Fear of Uncertainty by Muniya S. Khanna,

PhD, and Deborah Roth Ledley, PhD (Instant Help, 2018)

Something Bad Happened: A Kid's Guide to Coping With Events in the News by Dawn Huebner (Jessica Kingsley Publishers, 2019)

Coping Skills for Kids Workbook: Over 75 Coping Strategies to Help Kids Deal with Stress, Anxiety and Anger by Janine Halloran (PESI Publishing & Media, 2018)

1-Minute Gratitude Journal: A Kid's Guide to Finding the Good in Every Day (Tommy Nelson, 2021)

Books for Parents

Helping Your Anxious Child: A Step-by-Step Guide for Parents by Ronald M. Rapee, PhD; Ann Wignall, D.Psych; Susan H. Spence, PhD; Vanessa Cobham, PhD; and Heidi Lyneham, PhD (New Harbinger Publications, 2008)

Anxiety-Free Kids: An Interactive Guide for Parents and Children by Bonnie Zucker, PsyD (Prufrock Press, 2016)

Anxiety Relief for Kids: On-the-Spot Strategies to Help Your Child Overcome Worry, Panic, and Avoidance by Bridget Flynn Walker, PhD (New Harbinger Publications, 2017)

Acknowledgments

Great thanks to Andrea Lucado, Laura Helweg, Karen Hill, and Laura Minchew. They are the reason this book exists. I'm grateful beyond words to each of them.

LIFE COMES WITH A LOT OF QUESTIONS ... BUT JUST ONE ANSWER.

MAX LUCADO

ONE
GOD
ONE
PLAN
ONE
LIFE

A 365 STUDENT DEVOTIONAL

You've only got one life. And there's only one God who can make that life into something amazing.

Titles for Teens by Max Lucado

YOU WERE MADE TO
MAKE A DIFFERENCE

3:16 THE NUMBERS OF
HOPE, FOR TEENS

UNSHAKABLE HOPE PROMISE
BOOK, STUDENT EDITION

IT'S NOT ABOUT ME,
TEEN EDITION

MAKE EVERY DAY COUNT,
TEEN EDITION